Fertile Ground: Faith and Work

(FIELD GUIDE)

For Youth Pastors

Edited by Luke Bobo

Made to Flourish
10901 Lowell Avenue
Overland Park, Kansas 66210
madetoflourish.org
communications@madetoflourish.org

Cover design and creative direction: Eric Rivier
Interior design: Daniel Carroll and Eric Rivier

ISBN 9781696743884

Printed in the United States of America
First Edition

Contents

Introduction

Most young people in your youth group probably can't articulate who they want to become, but we all know the feeling. We all know what it is like to wrestle with our identity, beliefs, and the opinions of others. Young people today face insurmountable pressure to succeed, whether in sports, school, relationships, or future plans.

These years can be some of the most tumultuous years of a person's life because of these pivotal decisions and the pressure to conform to those around you. It's a season of becoming, for better or worse. One thing that remained steady in my life, though, was youth pastors and small group leaders who invested time, energy, and prayer into my life as a young adult. I look back and know I am who I am in part because of their investment.

As youth navigate what it means to be human, how to interact with their peers and parents in a healthy way, and learn what confidence in their own skin looks like, young people need steady leaders who help them answer questions about identity, morality, and their vocational future. In middle school, I didn't realize it at the time, but the youth pastors, small group leaders, and adults other than my parents changed the trajectory of my life. Your influence is powerful as a youth pastor, and you get the opportunity to speak into a young person's life in a unique way as someone who holds and expounds truth, goodness, and beauty to their souls in a chaotic season of growing up and becoming who God intended for them to be.

This collection of essays is the work of several men and women who believe your calling as a youth pastor is pivotal to the growth and development of young disciples in your church. We pray these essays help you as you wear the many hats of youth ministry, including the hats of guidance counselor, theologian, cultural facilitator, psychologist, and liturgist. They explore several theological and practical aspects of youth ministry and how to guide youth to better connect their own faith with school, future work, and relationships. Becoming who God intended for us to be is a lifelong endeavor that is best walked alongside others. We pray this book is a helpful tool toward that goal.

RuthAnne Irvin

Managing Editor, Made to Flourish

Youth Pastor as Theologian

BY NATHAN MILLER

> "In order to build a biblical-theological framework for understanding God's mission, the church's mission, and the church's mission to the nations, one must first understand the unified biblical narrative, including its four major plot movements—creation, fall, redemption, and restoration."[1] *Bruce Riley Ashford*

TEACHER OF GOD

The most obvious and hopefully well-worn hat youth pastors wear is *theologian* or *teacher of God*. In his letter to the Ephesians, the Apostle Paul explains what we do, "So Christ himself gave the... pastors and teachers, to equip his people for works of service, so that the body of Christ may be built up until we all reach unity in the faith and in the knowledge of the Son of God and become mature, attaining to the whole measure of the fullness of Christ," (Eph 4:11-13).[2] This means our faithful teaching as youth pastors is part of God's design to equip students for "works of service," and these "works" in turn unite and build up the Church to maturity and fullness in Christ. We teach about God "so that we may present everyone fully mature in Christ" (Col 1:28).

We teach toward maturity in our students and Paul further clarifies in Ephesians that maturity means "we will grow to become in every respect the mature body of him who is the head, that is, Christ" (Eph 4:15). The words "in every respect" mean our students' maturity should extend to every aspect of their lives both in and outside of the church. Therefore, the scope of our discipleship should match the scope of where God deserves glory — in *all* activity of a student's life. The more we help our students make connections between their faith and all their daily activity, the better equipped they will be at "doing it all for the glory of God" (1 Cor 10:31).

We call this "whole-life discipleship" or living all of life all for Christ. We want to train students to shape culture outside the four walls of the church, embodying their faith in the classroom and on the sports field, in their homes, and at their part-time jobs.[3] It is precisely in those settings or arenas outside of church where students most demonstrate their reliance on the Holy Spirit's power, contribute to human flourishing, and advance God's mission in the world.

In order for this to happen, we need to believe and teach a robust theology that is integral with all of life. Since our students live the majority of their lives away from youth group or the church, we must equip them to live out their faith brightly and clearly in those spaces. God did not make our students flashlights to only add a few more lumens to the youth room on Wednesday, but rather to illuminate every shadowy space in their school, neighborhood, or job with a holy brightness that elicits worship and gives glory to God (Matt 5:14-16).

THEOLOGY OF WORK

So how do we teach toward this kind of maturity? It requires a theology of work and vocation. John Stott defines work as "the expenditure of energy (manual or mental or both) in the service of others, which brings fulfillment to the worker, benefit to the community, and glory to God."[4] As we all engage in the social and cultural activity of work, we participate in the economy, this interrelated web of relationships that involve the giving and exchanging of goods and services. Our daily contribution to work and this broader economy is the primary platform by which we follow God's greatest command to love him and our neighbors as ourselves (Matt 22:36-40).[5]

Addressing work theologically with students acknowledges the background noise of questions they and their parents are already asking — What am I in school for? Which college, if any, should I attend? What do I want to do with my life? What is God calling you to do? How are you going to make a living? How are you going to afford college or trade school? — and enables you to speak God's truth into this critical area of life. Instead of building a youth group of Peter Pans, we celebrate adult responsibility[6] and "ordinary work" by inviting adults to talk about their jobs and how their faith animates their work. Through formal teaching and informal conversations, we help students clarify their vocation.

Vocation is derived from the Latin word *vox*, meaning "voice" or "vocal" and means "one's entire life lived in response to God's voice, or call." It can be used synonymously with "calling" from the Greek root *kaleo*, which adds a dimension "to give name to" or "to receive name from." In other words, these terms are about identity (who we are) and belonging (to whom we belong), and less about what we do.[7] Calling has deep theological roots[8] and we need to help our students understand and live in obedience to God's calling (vocation) for their lives.

PRIMARY AND SECONDARY CALLINGS

Here is where we must distinguish between primary and secondary callings. The former is what we all share as believers in Jesus, the latter is specific to an individual, based on the unique gifts God has given someone. Our primary calling is corporate, general, ordinary, and clear, while our secondary calling is individual, particular, special, and often mysterious.[9] Our primary vocation is to the Lord Jesus Christ (Rom 8:28-30). Os Guinness writes, "Our primary calling as followers of Christ is by him, to him, and for him. First and foremost we are called to Someone (God), not something (such as motherhood, politics, or teaching) or to somewhere (such as the inner city or Outer Mongolia)."[10]

For example, Jesus, as our "good shepherd" (John 10:11) "calls his own sheep by name and leads them out ... [and] my sheep listen to my voice; I know them, and they follow me" (John 10:3, 27). To be called by God is to be his sheep. This is our primary calling, to listen to the voice of the shepherd and follow him, since we are his. Our primary calling dictates our view of our work and the performance of work. We are to do them both with excellence (Col 3:23-25). We are to steward our vocations well and develop them, recognizing that in our work, we display God to the world.[11]

We need to teach students that all their secondary callings (as students, siblings, part-time workers, band members, etc.) are in response to God's primary calling. Some secondary callings can change, depending on the season of life, and demand Spirit sensitivity for guidance and direction. Students need not stress if they are confused about their secondary calling, since God has already made clear their first vocation is to behave as a follower of Christ. As they "seek first their heavenly Father's kingdom," things like secondary calling clarity will be given to them as well (Matt 6:33).

As youth pastors, we must also police language and not allow conversations about vocation to elevate salaries over substance. All work offered to God can be "true and proper worship" (Rom 12:1), regardless of the paycheck it earns. We should lead with a posture of curiosity and abundance, recognizing our diverse students will take up diverse secondary callings. As Dorothy Sayers argues, "Work is not primarily a thing one does to live, but the thing one lives to do. It is, or it should be, the full expression of the worker's faculties, the thing in which he finds spiritual, mental, and bodily satisfaction, and the medium in which he offers himself to God."[12]

We offer our work to God, but for the benefit of our neighbor. In other words, we love through our work. Work becomes a gift we give to others out of the grace we have received from God. Our work is not a means to earn God's favor, but an opportunity to pay it forward to our neighbor the favor God already lavishes on us in his grace. This is Paul's point in Ephesians 2:8-10. God saves us through grace, not our work. And as God's handiwork, he has prepared for each of us specific good work within our secondary callings that he will use through us to bless the world.

STORYTELLER

This brings us to an important point in our theology of vocation/ calling and work. As we have argued, if we desire maturity in our students that extends to their whole lives, we must teach a robust

Calling has *deep theological roots* and we need to help our students understand and live in *obedience to God's calling* (vocation) for their lives.

We offer our —
but for the
neighbor.
we love through

Work becomes
to others out
have received

work to God,
benefit of our
In other words,
our work.

<u>a gift</u> we give
of the grace we
from God.

<u>NATHAN MILLER</u>

theology of faith and work. But the only way to accomplish this with integrity to our own vocations as youth pastors is to believe it is central to the grand story of Scripture. If it is a side issue that only appears in select "cherry-picked" verses, then to focus on this within our ministries would be a distraction to our calling.

However, if Steven Garber is right when he writes "vocation is integral, not incidental, to the *missio Dei* (God's mission),"[13] then we must help our students see how God's grand mission in the world is directly connected with how our students spend their days (their work in and outside the classroom). We must be convinced that from start to finish, God cares deeply about the integration of faith and work and intends our students to grow to maturity in living out that integration in their lives.

Perhaps a better name for our theologian/teacher hat as youth pastors is *storyteller*, since it is the chief job of the youth pastor to tell the biblical story in such a faithful way that students not only see God clearly, but also see themselves as participants within the grand story.[14] How we tell the story is key.

As a father of five little children, reading stories has become a part-time job. On nights when I am tired and try abridging a story, skipping a page here or there, my kids see through it instantly. "You missed a page, Daddy!" they insist, wanting the whole story with all the details. Most sacred are those beginnings and endings.

The same temptation exists for youth pastors to tell an abridged story of the Christian faith. Whether it is our own laziness to "correctly handle the word of truth" (2 Tim 2:15) or a naiveté about the grand biblical narrative, many youth workers omit key parts of the scriptural story, leaving an incomplete and immature theology of faith and work. We must tell the whole story and not let our students miss those juicy, life-transforming details, especially in the bookends of Scripture.

FOUR-CHAPTER GOSPEL

Telling the whole story of Scripture means beginning in Genesis and ending in Revelation. It means telling the four-chapter gospel[15] (creation, fall, redemption, consummation), not just the two-chapter gospel (fall, redemption). The temptation for many youth pastors is to skip to Jesus and only talk about his saving us from our sin, but the Bible doesn't begin at Romans 3:23 (fall) and end at John 3:16 (redemption). Rather, Scripture opens with God's creation (Gen 1-2) and ends with God's new creation (Rev 21-22); both realms of God's activity he intends for our study and application.

Dutch theologian Herman Bavinck provides a helpful summary of Christianity that includes all four chapters of this grand biblical narrative: "God the Father has reconciled His created but fallen world through the death of His Son, and renews it into a Kingdom of God by His Spirit."[16]

Without a proper treatment of creation and consummation, students will not give God the glory he deserves as the ultimate worker in his original creation design and his new creation remodel of the cosmos. We need to see this grand view that "God is acting in history for the salvation of the world."[17] And while we often shy away from these bookends of Scripture for a number of reasons (e.g., difficult or confusing genre and content), Andy Crouch reminds us to trust the Scripture writers even here, because the central chapters (books) are trustworthy.[18] Let us walk briefly through this grand story, highlighting some of the details that form a mature theology of work.

GOD'S GRAND STORY

Creation

Among the key reasons we must begin in Genesis 1 is to recover the cultural mandate, which is what God gave Adam and Eve in Genesis 1:26-28. "Then God said, 'Let us make mankind in our image'... So God created mankind in his own image ... and said to them, 'Be fruitful and increase in number; fill the earth and subdue it. Rule over the fish in the sea and the birds in the sky and over every living creature that moves on the ground.'"

In these original marching orders from God, which continues through today, God invites humanity into a "Great Assignment"[19] of joining God in making something of this world. God provides the raw material in the six days of creation, and then invites us, as his image-bearers, to turn the good of creation into the very good of culture. In Genesis 1 we learn that a creative, working, ruling God created humans to likewise create, work, and rule, since we share his image. God elevates our everyday work by modeling from the beginning that such activity was not beneath his holy hands.[20]

Unlike the rulers of ancient times, who fashioned statues or idols in their own image and spread them throughout their territory to claim their dominion, God chose his people. He crafted them in his image and sends them throughout the world to declare his rule and reign. As unique and precious images of God our king, one of our primary purposes in life is to communicate to the watching world, through our lives, that God rules here. As we spread out into every vocational sphere and geographical region of the globe, people should see God's ruling activity over that area. In this sense, ruling becomes the day-in-day-out activity of working with creativity in the world.

An important question to ask our students is "What is your garden? How is God calling you to bring forth flourishing within that garden? How do we harness, manipulate, craft, and utilize the raw materials of our domains to the benefit of others?" We should all be intent on leaving a trail of flourishing wherever we go. John Mark Comer explains:

> As people made in God's image, we can join him in
> this ongoing creative work. As his partners, we can

> reshape the raw materials of his world in such a way
> that people see the beauty behind the beauty ... We
> can't make the world—but we can remake it into a
> macchiato, a building, an app, a dress, a book, a meal,
> a school, a cure, a song, a business, or ten thousand
> other things in such a way that for those with eyes to
> see ... they are glaring and inescapable.[21]

Moses, who penned the creation account, was likely reflecting on the weighty responsibility of the cultural mandate and our holy call to work when he wrote Psalm 90:17: "May the favor of the Lord our God rest on us; establish the work of our hands for us — yes, establish the work of our hands."

Another point to emphasize with students is how God has uniquely gifted them with his image and a particular set of skills to accomplish his purposes. Made in the image of a triune God, we are wired for relationship and need community to represent God to the world. Bill Hendricks calls our giftedness an "incarnational truth." He explains that when God designs each human, "He takes some dimension of Himself that He does in an infinite way and fashions a human being to do that exact same thing, only in a finite way. So when a person does the thing that God has designed them to do, they mirror for the rest of us a dimension of God that we otherwise would never get to see."[22]

Fall

If the creation chapter of God's grand story is the way things should be, the fall explains the way the world currently is. Life in Eden was marked by *shalom*, "the Old Testament word for peace, meaning the rich, integrated, relational wholeness God intends for his creation."[23] Another name for Eden could have been "Immanuel," because God dwelled there in intimate fellowship with humanity, walking, and communing with Adam and Eve (Gen 3:8). Adam and Eve whistled while they worked, fulfilling their "Great Assignment" of tending the garden, naming the animals, and being at peace with self, others, God, and the created order.

Then a serpent tempted them to question God's command regarding a forbidden tree of knowing good and evil (Gen 2:17; 3:1-5) and they chose autonomy over humility, rejecting God's gracious ordering of things in Genesis 3.[24] Their mutinous act shattered the *shalom* of creation, leaving a rift in all the major relationships of life — with self, with God, with others, and with the created order. Of the many consequences, shame now pervades the human psyche (self), communion with God is broken (God), their marriage would be riddled with struggle (others), Eve would suffer pain in childbirth, and Adam and Eve's work would be filled with frustration (created order). In his grace, God represses a full unraveling and undoing of his creation, by containing the damage and promising a solution through Eve's offspring (Gen 3:15).

Students need to see that God established work before the fall. Work, and having the ability to work, are still good gifts of the Lord. But our work is now frustrating. Farmers may plant corn but reap little. Work can be unnecessarily arduous because our coworkers can be annoying (along with us). But work is still a gift. We image God when we work and rest. However, like most good gifts, work can become the ultimate thing. In other words, we can err in two extreme ways: We can think less of our work (which leads to sloth and wastefulness) or we can think too much of our work (which leads to idolatry).[25]

We should ask our students questions about their work to diagnose where they land on the spectrum from lazy to overworked so we can shepherd them appropriately. We can also ask them where they see the fall in their work, helping point out the lack of shalom that God's kingdom has come to fix.

Redemption

Thanks to the glorious arrival of the True Adam, who followed God's ordering of things and died in our place, we now have access to redemption — "In him we have redemption through his blood, the forgiveness of sins, in accordance with the riches of God's grace" (Eph 1:7; Col 1:14). This chapter in God's Grand Story describes how life "can be," for those who participate in God's redemptive activity in the world.

Jesus' redemption is not only for individual salvation, but corporate and cosmic as well. The gospel of Jesus Christ unleashes a great redemption project we are invited into. Through the power of the Spirit, we are being "conformed to the image of his Son" (Rom 8:28) and God's grand project to reestablish shalom. Theologian Haley Goranson Jacob explains that when Paul used this phrase in Romans 8, he means that our salvation in Christ recreates us back to our original function of having dominion over the earth, but no longer in a failed way because of our sin. Instead, we return to ruling creation and representing God to the world, but now through Christ and his example of sacrificial love, service, and peace.[26]

God desires to renew all things in Christ. In Romans 8, Paul expresses the longing we feel waiting for God to finally restore what he's begun to restore in Jesus, "We know that the whole creation has been groaning as in the pains of childbirth right up to the present time. Not only so, but we ourselves, who have the firstfruits of the Spirit, groan inwardly as we wait eagerly for our adoption to sonship, the redemption of our bodies" (Rom 8:22-23).

If salvation was only individual, why would Paul mention its cosmic scope? Indeed all creation laments the lack of shalom. Students need to see beyond their private salvation and ask, "What is my salvation for? The answer..."for the life of the world."[27] As Chris Wright explains:

The Bible itself will correct our tendency to reduce the gospel to a solution to our individual sin problem and a swipe card for heaven's door, and replace that reductionist impression with a message that has to do with the cosmic reign of God in Christ that will ultimately eradicate evil from God's universe (and solve our individual sin problem too, of course)."[28]

Youth pastors may feel ill-equipped to talk with certain students whose interests are outside the pastors' own experiences or interests. Recruiting diverse leadership helps, but so does this theological framework for ministry. We should be able to make connections with our students about any interest by directly connecting that interest to its spiritual significance in God's kingdom purposes. There is a direct correlation between every hobby, extra-curricular activity, sport, or student club and God's grand purpose in the world. There are no "throw-away" involvements if God's promise to renew all of creation is true. Finding these connections, correlations, and extrapolations is the heart of vibrant student discipleship. What better job is there than helping students discover not only what they love, but how God is working to restore what they love to its original, perfected version? And especially how their lives may be part of God's restoration project.

We need to help our students see how _God offers a foretaste of heaven_ even now in this broken creation.

Consummation

In the final chapters of Revelation, we are promised a "new heaven and a new earth." This picture of creation restored makes up the final chapter in the Four-Chapter Gospel and describes the way life will be. Consider this glorious description:

> ...and a voice will say, "Look! God's dwelling place is now among the people, and he will dwell with them. They will be his people, and God himself will be with them and be their God. He will wipe every tear from their eyes. There will be no more death or mourning or crying or pain, for the old order of things has passed away." He who was seated on the throne said, "I am making everything new!" (Rev 21:3-5).

Just as Jesus conquered death at his resurrection, when he returns, he will defeat all of death's effects by giving us new, resurrected bodies. Quoting Isaiah 25:8, Paul describes our new bodies in 1 Corinthians, "When the perishable has been clothed with the imperishable, and the mortal with immortality, then the saying that is written will come true: "Death has been swallowed up in victory" (1 Cor 15:54).

We need to help our students see how God offers a foretaste of heaven even now in this broken creation. As chef and Episcopalian priest, Robert Farrar Capon, explains, "Half of earth's gorgeousness lies hidden in the glimpsed city it longs to become ... and it is our glory to see it so and thirst until Jerusalem comes home at last. We were given appetites, not to consume the world and forget it, but to taste its goodness and hunger to make it great."[29] In this way, we need to help students see how the already, but not yet pattern of promises of God's kingdom apply in their daily work as well.[30]

We also need to help students see that things won't be destroyed, but refined, since in the new heavens, "the glory and honor of the nations will be brought into it" (Rev 21:26). If we compare how God deals with his original creation, as well as us, every time we sin, it is outside of God's character to annihilate, but to restore. James Hamilton explains:

> God has not trashed his first failed attempt and started over. To the contrary, what he set out to do when he made this world he will bring about when he makes it new. God will make the world new, and we will do new work. The new work we will do is the work of ruling and subduing, working and keeping, exercising dominion and rendering judgment, all as God's people in God's place in God's way.[31]

If God promises to restore all the dimensions that were broken at the fall, a helpful exercise for students is to point out the four fundamental life relationships (with self, with God, with others, and with the created order) that God will make right again and reflect on these marks of the consummated kingdom.[32] We should also study the life of Christ and his healings with this kingdom mindset. Ask students how Jesus and his apostles' miracles undid the effects of the fall and brought kingdom glimpses of ultimate restoration.

CONCLUSION

This brief survey of the grand biblical narrative shows us that work and vocation are central to our calling as Christians. If we are going to take our role of shepherding young people as seriously as Jesus expects us to, we must approach discipleship holistically. This Four-Chapter Story approach provides students a theology that connects their curricular and extracurricular endeavors with God's foundational plan for the world. Albert Wolters explains:

> If we see that human history and the unfolding of
> culture and society are integral to creation and its
> development, that they are not outside God's plans
> for the cosmos, despite the sinful aberrations, but
> rather were built in from the beginning, were part of
> the blueprint that we never understood before, then
> we will be much more open to the positive possibil-
> ities for service to God in such areas as politics and
> the film arts, computer technology and business
> administration, developmental economics,
> and skydiving.[33]

We must help students see this more complete view of life, set out in the Scriptures, that connects God's mission in the world to all that happens both inside and outside of youth group. We need to give students this grander picture of what the gospel of Jesus Christ accomplishes, not just for them individually, but for all of creation. In other words, how students spend their time at school, work, and extracurricular activities matters for the king-dom of God.

If a student's primary calling is to bring glory to Jesus by obey-ing and following him with their lives, ask students if they are liv-ing at the nexus of the great assignment (cultural mandate) (Gen 1:28), the great commandment (Matt 22:36-40), and the great com-mission (Matt 28:18-20). By living in Spirit-empowered obedience to these three umbrella commands of God, a student can be con-fident they are living out their primary calling, as we help them discern their secondary callings. We make disciples *and* we make something of the world, and these dual acts demonstrate our love for God and neighbor. As Comer explains, "Discipleship is about learning how to become a good human being. And how to live into *both* your callings, to make disciples *and* to create culture."[34]

When we tell the whole story and address the whole student, we are positioned to help our young people answer their most pressing questions like "What am I supposed to do with my life?" In answering these questions of calling and vocation, we help them reach maturity in Christ for all of life.

REFLECTION QUESTIONS:

1. How have you thought about your vocation as a youth pastor? Have you sinned through idleness or making it an idol?
2. Have you ever affirmed the vocation of your students through celebration or commissioning?
3. How might you strengthen your ability to prepare students for their "works of service" within their vocations?
4. Have you been teaching a two-chapter or four-chapter gospel?
5. What practical steps can you take today to help your students understand these big picture ideas?

———

Nathan Miller is the senior high pastor at Grace Point Church in New Brighton, Minnesota, and a City Network Leader for Made to Flourish in the Twin Cities. Nathan lives with his wife, Maria, and their five children in Mounds View, Minnesota. You can follow him on Instagram @nathanleemiller.

Youth Pastor as Guidance Counselor

BY PAUL BRANDES

"What if learning to have the 'mind of Christ' was less like memorizing a map and more like learning how to live and move and have our being in Christ? How can we form and educate young people so that they know the gospel in their bones? What if we could absorb a biblical understanding of the world like we were natives of God's good creation? What if education weren't first and foremost about what we know but about what we love?"[35] *James K.A. Smith*

I began considering pastoral ministry when I was a junior in high school. Specifically, I sensed a call to youth ministry, in part because of the positive influence of both my middle and high school pastors. *I want to do for others what Brandon and Dan did for me,* I thought.

By the beginning of my senior year, I was convinced of the path that lay ahead: college at a Christian institution to study the Bible, seminary training, and then the pastorate. Only one pesky detail remained before my perfect plan: another year of high school.

The sad truth, as I reflect on it now, is that my "Sunday to Monday gap" significantly widened upon my decision to pursue pastoral ministry. My faith convictions professed on Sunday didn't inform my work on Monday. In other words, I was perpetuating what is far too common in the church: the disconnect between my faith and my work, which at the time consisted of history and English classes.

Consequently, I was less motivated during my senior year. I developed a dangerous attitude toward my education, thinking, "What will I need calculus for when I'm serving God as a youth pastor?" I thought I was honoring God by answering a call to serve him as a pastor, but instead I was dishonoring him by ignoring his call to serve him as a student.

The reality for students, from kindergarten to grad school and beyond, is that their primary workplace is school. So often, however, Christian students don't view school as a calling, as an arena for meaningful and sacred work. Instead, school is at best a utilitarian means to an end, and at worst a mandated sentence.

Now, maybe you disagree with naming a student's schooling their work, with the argument that it is a sacred and high calling. After all, since school is compulsory in many countries around the globe, middle and high school aged students do not have a choice of whether or not to participate in their education. And isn't there some measure of choice involved with our callings? Isn't it that we experience an existential feeling or leading that we identify as a "call" and then respond to it?

Here, Os Guinness is helpful in reframing our understanding of calling by breaking it down into primary and secondary callings, which are deeply interconnected. Remember as Nathan Miller pointed out in Chapter 1, that each and every Christian is first called to Christ, by Christ, and for Christ. Importantly, we are called first to someone, rather than to something or to somewhere.

But, we should not forget that when Christ calls us, he does so decisively. So much so that "everything we are, everything we do, and everything we have is invested with a special devotion and dynamism lived out as a response to his summons and service."[36]

These responses to God's summons become our secondary callings. And notice that there is no language of choice within the definition. Certainly, some of our secondary callings are received by choice (under this framework of calling, even hobbies we choose to engage are secondary callings, opportunities to respond to and honor God), but others are not. I have secondary callings as a son to David and Janice and as a brother to Annie, but I chose neither of them.

We also are aided by Guinness' distinction between special and ordinary secondary callings:

> A special calling refers to tasks and missions laid on individuals through a direct, specific, supernatural communication from God. Ordinary calling, on the other hand, is the believer's sense of life-purpose and life-task in response to God's primary call, 'follow me,' even when there is no direct, supernatural communication from God about a secondary calling. ... In this sense, no follower of Christ is without a calling, for we all have an original calling even if we do not all have a later, special calling.[37]

So it goes for the middle school student, for what calling is more ordinary than sixth period science class? And though school is an ordinary secondary calling not chosen, a secondary calling it remains — a massive opportunity for the student to invest in God's kingdom with devotion and dynamism.

However, it is unlikely that the middle and high school students in our youth groups will have felt a sense of calling to school. Therefore, as youth pastors, we need to see it as a key part of our work to help them bring a robust sense of calling to their education.

In this endeavor, it will serve us to consider ourselves as guidance counselors, a job my father has done faithfully and fruitfully for the past 20 years. He uses a guiding framework of three areas of focus for their high school years: involvement, relationships, and academics.

How might this framework aid us in our work as youth pastors? I'm convinced all three arenas demand our attention, but our role in the academic life of our students likely needs the most work.

INVOLVEMENT

For my father in this area, he asked his students to get involved with something (sports, theatre, music, clubs), so they feel connected to the school and are part of something bigger than themselves.

Isn't that part of our task as well — to connect middle and high school students to something bigger than themselves? In our work, we connect not to a school, but to God's Big Story. As Christians, our firm belief is that God is on a mission to make all things new again, and incredibly, we get to play a (small) role in that work. What a privilege! Are we being diligent in this aspect of *our* work, encouraging students to find themselves in God's story?

We need to help students "play to their strengths and interests" through God-centered conversations. Diagnostic questions like "What has God wired you to enjoy? Why do you think God has put that passion in your heart? You seem to have a God-given ability to excel in that school subject, what might that mean for your future?" should become a part of our tool belt in our work with students.

RELATIONSHIPS

Students need education about not only Algebra each week, but also the dangers of isolation and the importance of asking for help when needed. We were not made to navigate the complexities of life alone. In addition, we need to consider connecting this relational conversation to calling. Remember, we are first called to *someone*, not to *something* or *somewhere*. Are we regularly reminding our students of their primary calling to Christ, by Christ, and for Christ? Are we painting a compelling picture to them of the importance of making God their first relationship? Placing the conversation of the importance of their relationship with God in the domain of *calling* provides an easy bridge to the interconnectedness between our primary and secondary callings.

ACADEMICS

I'll be the first youth pastor to admit that for too long, I thought I held no role to play in the academic lives of my students. Maybe if you pressed me I would have said something about how I encourage my students to work hard in their classes with integrity, to be respectful to their teachers, to be nice to their fellow classmates. These are good and right admonitions — and certainly are connections of their faith to their schooling. But I would have stopped there. However, I now have come to believe there is much more to say.

The question that sent me down the road of this line of thinking was a simple one: What is the ultimate goal of education? Perhaps I hadn't seriously considered this question before because the answer seems self-evident. The ultimate goal of education is to impart knowledge previously unknown.

Or is it? Diving into the history of education reveals different answers have been offered to this question. Maybe the ultimate goal of education is to learn how to learn. Or maybe it's to create "good" citizens who can contribute positively to society.

...we are first called to _someone_, not to _something_ or _somewhere_. Are we regularly reminding our students of their primary calling to Christ, by Christ, and for Christ?

Perhaps the ultimate goal of education _is_ to impart knowledge, because knowledge of the truth leads to freedom. Indeed, _liber_, the root of "liberal learning" (which in the West is the learning that the bulk of our students experience) is the Latin word for _free_. Gene Fant Jr. helpfully defines liberal learning as being "aimed at a breadth of knowledge that [includes] a wide range of subjects that [train] the mind to analyze challenges and formulate solutions or to anticipate future opportunities and strategies."[38]

But he also insightfully reminds us we need to step back and ask, "From what does liberal learning free us, and for what purpose are we then free?"[39] Unsurprisingly, this question has also resulted in different answers throughout the centuries. The Christian response is that a proper liberal arts education frees one from self and from egotism. However, as Fant Jr. continues, "The post-Enlightenment, secular vision of liberal learning exalts a freedom, instead, from the tyranny of institutions and social structures that would circumscribe our lives, freeing us so that we may follow our hearts and minds wherever they may wish to roam."[40]

Furthermore, as Thomas Hine shows in *The Rise and Fall of the American Teenager*, different groups of people will answer the question about the ultimate goal of education in a variety of ways. Speaking specifically of secondary education, he writes,

> Schoolmen might proclaim in speeches and editorials the ability of public education to realize democracy by preventing caste. Parents, however, usually see this issue differently. They hope that their children's schooling will at least preserve their position within the class system, or even better, enhance it. Parents aren't all that interested in democracy. They're looking not for equality but for an advantage.[41]

All of this adds up to a rather muddy picture about the ultimate goal of education. And that is where I think youth pastors have an important role to play in the academic arena of their student's lives. What if the picture didn't have to be muddy? What if the biblical worldview could offer a compelling answer to our question? And what if we saw it as part of our duty to contextualize that answer in a convincing manner to our students? What if we introduced them to the proper *telos* or goal of their education early?

Fant Jr. submits that "the primary purpose of education is the glorification of God [which] typically finds an overflow in the edification of his people, whether the people of faith or humanity as a created race."[42] In other words, the Christian view of education is that it exists for the broad formation of humanity so we might better glorify God. The phrase "broad formation" is key, because it is, of course, possible for Christians to become myopic in their view of formation, thereby slipping into the "education is ultimately about information transfer" fallacy.

But as James K. A. Smith argues in *You Are What You Love*, true formation occurs at the level of our *loves*, not at the level of our *knowledge*. Connecting this idea to education, Smith writes, "Formation is an inherently educational project ... but this also means that education is an inherently formational project, not just an informational endeavor."[43]

He continues, explaining more of Fant Jr.'s point about the ultimate purpose of a Christian education:

> While I can absolutely be an engineer or musician or financial analyst "to the glory of God," I need to consider the ultimate ends to which my work is going to be oriented. A Christian education can never be merely a mastery of a field of knowledge or technical skills; learning is embedded in a wider vision of who I am called to be and what God is calling the world to be. How does my learning fit in this Story? And what practices will cultivate this ultimate orientation in me?[44]

We must not miss that a Christian education is possible, even for those students who attend "secular" middle and high schools. The difference is that those institutions will not work to connect those dots for their students, and indeed at times may even actively work against imbedding their student's learning in God's Big Story. However, that does not mean it isn't possible for a Christian student to see their "secular" education as an important part of their formation into a more faithful and fruitful follower of Jesus whose ultimate goal is to glorify God.

Admittedly, this is an audacious task. It won't be accomplished in one night of youth group, or even one whole year of student ministry programming. And it certainly won't be accomplished without bringing our student's parents into this conversation!

But challenging as it may be, I'm convinced of its worthiness.

And in those conversations where students complain about school, or during those nights of youth group where the conversation drifts toward everyone's least favorite teachers, I will trust that the Holy Spirit is doing a work I cannot see, and I will rest in the wise words from my father regarding his guidance counseling work with high school students: "My first rule of thumb is to take the long view."

THE PROBLEM OF SUBSTANDARD EDUCATION

We would be remiss if we did not mention the myriad of students, who for whatever reason, receive a substandard education. This is a real problem, and ignoring it only perpetuates the dilemma and its effects. Youth pastors can't solve this on their own, but we can create an oasis of excellence in our sphere of influence, which is to say that we can make a real difference in the lives of the students in our youth groups who don't receive the education they deserve.

Educate yourself on the schools that are represented in your youth group. Where are they strong and where are they weak? What is their history? Who leads them? How involved are parents in the life of the schools?

If the public schools represented in your youth group are substandard, what other options (homeschooling, private, charter, etc.) do families explore? Are families even able to explore other options? Being able to choose something other than the public school system is often a sign of great privilege.

If families are not able to choose, how could you and your church begin to stand in the gap? Think creatively. Get up stream a bit: Is there a reading program at the elementary school level that already exists that your church could partner with, mobilizing adult volunteers to help students learn this vital skill? Or what about a mentoring or tutoring program at the middle or high school level? If not, could you organize one that operates out of the church after school? Or maybe an informal homework club would be helpful, where students would have a place to come to get a jump start on homework in the church environment with a few trusted adults that could lend a hand.

What if your church launched a scholarship program that made it possible for some students to attend a different school, or for all students to participate in supplemental programs that would aid their education? What if you (or your lead pastor) ran for and served on the school board, not as an addition to your work as a pastor but as an integral part of it?

The problem of substandard education is a monster, and we won't solve it ourselves. But that doesn't mean we should resign ourselves (and therefore, the students in our youth groups) to the negative ripple effects that come from this problem. Indeed, through creativity, innovation, and the Holy Spirit, I believe we can make a difference.

CONCLUSION: PRACTICAL TIPS

I certainly don't have it all figured out, but here are three simple practices I'm integrating into my work with students. These are the beginnings of my attempts to guide my students toward seeing school as one of their secondary callings.

1. Celebrate school instead of disparaging it

This is the lowest hanging fruit available, in my opinion. How are students supposed to begin to catch a vision of the beauty of their schooling as a secondary calling if you, as their youth pastor, constantly bash it?

Students are often quick to complain about school — the difficult subject, the tough teacher, the early mornings, and on and on. In a well-intended effort to enter their world, youth pastors often subtly encourage this negative attitude toward school. Questions such as "What's your least favorite subject?" or "Show of hands, who's been caught this year texting in class?" can produce short-term wins ("My youth pastor gets it; school is the worst"), but they ultimately result in a long-term disconnect between students' faith and their work. Instead, youth pastors should acknowledge the real and frustrating challenges of school while seeking to convince students of its value by celebrating the parts that are good.

But to do this, you actually have to know the good parts: Is there a teacher they like and find compelling? A subject they're mastering? An extracurricular activity that's giving them life? Our job as youth pastors is to enter into their lives, ask good questions, and then celebrate those things with them.

2. Spend time in school with your students

This is akin to a workplace visit with adults, a trusted tool in the toolbelt of pastors seeking to help adults see their work as worship. Students may balk at this at first (like many adults do when I broach the subject with them), but here's a quick way to help them see value in these visits: "You come to the place where I work all the time! I'd love to return the favor and come visit where you get to work as you engage your schooling."

Practically, this could take on a lot of different forms. Many schools will allow you to eat lunch in the lunchroom with your students if you complete their visitor sign-in process. Or find out what sport teams your students are on and show up for games. Did you play a sport in high school or college? Consider volunteering as an assistant coach for the team of that sport at your local school. Do you have students in the play or musical? Be there on opening night to show your support. Or think big: Would it be the right leverage to serve as a substitute teacher one day out of your week? Maybe not, but again, the point is to think creatively as you implement this practice.

YOUTH PASTOR AS
GUIDANCE COUNSELOR

The Christian
view of education
is that it exists
for the broad
formation of
humanity so
we might better
glorify God.

PAUL BRANDES

3. Teach the idea of school as work

How well does your teaching prepare your students for what they spend the majority of their time doing? A series on different books of the Bible, and even many topical series common in youth groups (dating and sex, friendship, relating to your parents, technology), are worthy and helpful.

But the students in your youth group spend more than 40 hours a week engaged in their work of school. Isn't that worthy, too? Youth pastor, start small with a message from Colossians 3:23. Ask this driving question: "What if God were your teacher?" Sprinkle in stories from your own time as a student, and challenge students to see their schooling as one of the primary places they follow and obey Jesus.

CLOSING ACTIVITY

Gather a group of students from your youth group to facilitate a focus group about how they view their education. Here are some questions to get you started:

1. How do you view school? What has contributed to the view that you hold?
2. What do you think the ultimate purpose of your education is? How did you arrive at that answer?
3. What role does your faith play in your education? Would you describe your faith as *connected* or *disconnected* with your education? Why?
4. Do you find it easy to disconnect from your faith while you're at school?
5. What is good about school for you right now? What is hard and challenging?
6. How could I help support you in your education?

CLOSING ACTION

Choose one of the examples from the section on spending time in school with your students and put it into practice over the next month.

CLOSING REFLECTION QUESTION

How did you view your education as a middle and high school student? How does that background shape how you lead in this arena with your students today?

———

Paul Brandes serves college students as chaplain at his undergrad alma mater, Sterling College in Sterling, Kansas. He previously served in the local church as an executive pastor, associate pastor, and director of junior high ministries. He has over 10 years of student ministry experience.

Youth Pastor as Psychologist

BY MERYL HERR

"...I can define my identity only against a background of things that matter."[45] Charles Taylor

For me, the worst part of being a middle school math teacher had nothing to do with Algebra or teenage hormones. The worst part of being a middle school math teacher was obligatory attendance at the school band concert. Despite their best efforts to play in tune, the students' program of show tunes and movie themes often sounded worse to me than the screeching I endured while writing equations on the chalkboard.

As a musician, I appreciate the importance of being in tune. Being in tune is a little bit science and a little bit art. Each musical note, or pitch, that we hear has a certain frequency. When I play my guitar, I adjust the tension of each of my six strings so the right frequencies sound when I play a chord and strum.

When I want to play with other musicians, I have to make sure— I am in tune with them prior to making sure I am in tune with

myself. To do that, we use a tuning standard. If you have been
the symphony, you have probably heard the tuning standard
sound. A piano or oboe plays a note — often A 440Hz — and all
of the instruments tune to it. You may hear the violins, violas,
and cellos find the A, followed by the trumpets, saxophones,
and flutes. Then scales and arpeggios sound above the drone as
musicians check that they are in tune with themselves. If band
and orchestra members do not tune to one another, the result is
a cacophony.

For teens today, identity development has become more about
being in tune with oneself than being in tune with others. They want
to be authentic and original, attending to their own desires. Philosopher Charles Taylor captures the ethos of this pursuit, writing that
"Being true to myself means being true to my own originality, and
that is something only I can articulate and discover. [46] The result,
according to Taylor, is a Sinatra-esque "I did it my way" outlook: "It
is what gives sense to the idea of 'doing your own thing' or 'finding
your own fulfillment.'"[47]

Instead, Taylor argues, we can and should define ourselves in
relation to others and in connection to ideals greater than ourselves. He argues,

> I can define my identity only against the background
> of things that matter....Only if I exist in a world in which
> history, or the demands of nature, or the needs of my
> fellow human beings, or the duties of citizenship, or the
> call of God, or something else of this order *matters* cru-
> cially, can I define an identity for myself that is not trivial.
> Authenticity is not the enemy of demands that emanate
> from beyond the self; it supposes such demands.[48]

The Christian's quest for identity begins with being in tune with
God. Thomas À Kempis prayed his life would be ordered "to
[the] praise, glory, and eternal honor" of God.[49] The classic hymn

"Come Thou Fount of Every Blessing" echoes this sentiment in the line, "Tune my heart to sing Thy praise."[50]

How do we help today's teens tune to God before tuning to themselves? In other words, how do we help them understand their identity in Christ as they navigate other questions of identity? In this chapter, we will wear the hat of psychologists, seeking to help teens navigate the quest of identity development by encouraging them to find their fundamental identity in Christ.

THE QUEST FOR IDENTITY

"Who am I? Why am I here? What is life all about?" The search for the answers to life's big questions is a quest for identity, a quest for a sense of self that everyone struggles to understand. Jeffrey Jensen Arnett, an expert on emerging adulthood, says that emerging adults seek to "clarify their sense of who they are and what they want out of life."[51] One scholar describes adolescent development as teenagers discovering how they will contribute to production and reproduction in society.[52] In other words, in the process of developing their identity, adolescents will begin thinking about their future careers and romantic relationships.

Nowadays, the quest for identity often begins in late adolescence and continues into emerging adulthood.[53] And it is a quest often taken alone. According to developmental psychologists, "The transition [to adulthood] has become increasingly individualized, such that young people must largely define for themselves, and live up to, what it means to be an adult."[54] Today's teens often search for answers to life's big questions by themselves and for themselves.

The quest for identity leads to experimentation. Like young researchers, teens proceed through a version of the scientific method as they explore possible selves and try on different personas, observing what satisfies their longings and answers their questions. They may sign up for a new sport or pursue a

The book of Ecclesiastes reminds us we will never find our identity in the *choices we make*, in the *work that we do*.

new hobby. They might change their wardrobe, dye their hair, or pierce their bodies. They might become young workaholics trying to win all of the accolades or become young wallflowers hoping to go unnoticed. They might accentuate their solidarity with their cultural or ethnic group. They might experiment with drugs and alcohol, join a club or a gang, or attempt to become a YouTube or Instagram celebrity. As they are able, they will try on various personas or accentuate certain parts of themselves in search of acceptance, meaning, and purpose.[55]

How do we help teens clothe themselves with Christ daily *before* they try on these different personas? How do we help them experiment as faithful disciples of Jesus? We point them to one of the grandest experiments in the Bible and the important lessons about identity learned from it.

THE ECCLESIASTES EXPERIMENT

Ecclesiastes opens by introducing us to its main character: the teacher. And the teacher begins his story with a proclamation: "Meaningless! Meaningless!...Utterly meaningless! Everything is meaningless!" Work? Meaningless! Finding satisfaction? Meaningless! Making an impact that will be remembered by future generations? Meaningless. He sought answers to some of life's biggest questions and found their answers meaningless.

Could the teacher find meaning and purpose in the pleasures and pursuits of the world apart from God? Could he tune his life to something other than God? He wondered, and he devised an experiment to find out. He tried pleasure and found it meaningless. He tried wisdom, folly, and work. They, too, left him empty. At the end of his grand experiment, the teacher concluded that nothing could replace God as the proper center of his life. Without God at the center, everything in the world — from work to wisdom, from evil to injustice — was meaningless.

Therefore, he offered this advice to his students: "Remember your creator in the days of your youth" (Ecc 12:1). In other words, tune your life to God. The narrator of Ecclesiastes summarized the wisdom gained from the teacher's experiment: "Fear God and keep his commandments, for this is the duty of all mankind. For God will bring every deed into judgment, including every hidden thing, whether it is good or evil" (Ecc 12:13-14). The narrator, too, emphasized the importance of a God-centered life.

The book of Ecclesiastes reminds us we will never find our identity in the choices we make, in the work that we do. All of that is fleeting, or meaningless. Instead, we find our identity in God; God should be at the center of our lives. From the wisdom of Ecclesiastes, we discover four truths about our identity in Christ.

WE ARE INTENDED

The teacher in Ecclesiastes wanted his students to remember God created them (Ecc 12:1). God intended each of us. He planned our existence. He orchestrated the day of our birth and knows the day and the circumstances of our death. The psalmist declared to God, "Your eyes saw my unformed body; all the days ordained for me were written in our book before one of them came to be" (Ps 139:16).

The quest for identity leads to experimentation. _Like young researchers, teens proceed through a version of the scientific method_ as they explore possible selves and try on different personas, observing what satisfies their longings and answers their questions.

MERYL HERR

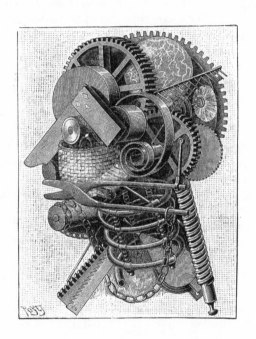

All of our days are not meaningless, though. God created us for a purpose. The Apostle Paul wrote, "For we are God's handiwork, created in Christ Jesus to do good works, which God prepared in advance for us to do" (Eph 2:10). God not only intended our lives but also intended the good works that he wants us to do while on earth. A life properly tuned to God recognizes he created us and "made us alive in Christ" so we can partner with Christ in his redemptive mission in the world (Eph 2:5).

WE ARE RESPONSIBLE

Since we were created *on* purpose and *for* a purpose, we bear a certain amount of responsibility by virtue of existing. To be human is to be responsible to God, our Creator. God gave the first humans the responsibility to care for and cultivate his creation: "Be fruitful and increase in number; fill the earth and subdue it. Rule over the fish in the sea and the birds in the sky and all the creatures that move along the ground" (Gen 1:28). In giving this command, God shared his rule with us. He calls us to responsible stewardship of his rule within our spheres of influence.

The writer of Ecclesiastes summarizes our responsibility: "fear God and keep his commandments" (Ecc 12:13). When we do not know precisely what responsible stewardship of God's rule looks like in a given situation, we can be certain of our call to fear him and obey him. Jesus put it this way to a religious leader in his day: "Love the Lord your God with all your heart and with all your soul and with all your mind....Love your neighbor as yourself" (Matt 22:37-39).

In his book, *Visions of Vocation*, Steven Garber describes how this sort of responsibility springs from our covenantal relationship with our Creator. We find ourselves caring about the world, and about the people in it, he argues. We find ourselves caring for causes. But why? "Why do we care?" he asks. "Because we see ourselves in relationship, 'obligated by the very fact of our existence.' And now knowing what we know, we are responsible, for love's sake, for the people and places that are ours—if we have eyes that see."[56]

WE ARE ACCOUNTABLE

Responsibility and accountability go hand-in-hand. Why do we take our responsibility to love God and love others seriously? The narrator of Ecclesiastes answers, "For God will bring every deed into judgment" (Ecc 12:14). Reading those words in light of our own teenage years may make us cower or cringe. We may recall the unkind words we wrote in a yearbook, the lipgloss we stole from the drugstore, the graffiti we scrawled on an overpass. Our minds rehearse a litany of our transgressions. But, in Christ, we know that, even in the face of judgment, we have free and full forgiveness for sins (Eph 1:7; Col 1:14; 1 John 2:1-2). Still, God holds us accountable for what we do with the responsibility he has given to us.

Jesus told a parable about responsibility and accountability (Matt 25:14-30). A man who was going on a journey gave his servants the responsibility of managing his wealth while he was gone. Two servants invested the money the man entrusted to them. The third did not. He buried his money in the ground. When the man returned, he was pleased with the servants who had made a return on their investment. He called the third wicked, lazy, and worthless and had him thrown out.

God has given us the responsibility of loving him and loving others. He has entrusted us with the care and cultivation of his creation, and he has also entrusted us with the gospel (1 Thess 2:4). God expects us to steward well our time, our talents, and our treasures — even if our treasures cannot be measured in dollars.

WE ARE TOGETHER

The responsibility and accountability outlined in Ecclesiastes 12:13-14 do not apply to only a few people. It applies to "all mankind." We share in this common identity as we rightly tune our lives to God.

Yet, togetherness does not necessarily imply sameness. Our responsibilities differ because God calls and equips us uniquely. The Apostle Paul reminded the Corinthian Christians of this reality when he described the differences between his work and Apollos' work among them: "I planted the seed, Apollos watered it, but God has been making it grow" (1 Cor 3:6). God had assigned them separate tasks even though those tasks shared the same purpose (1 Cor 3:5-9). Paul summarized their responsibility, accountability, and togetherness well: "The one who plants and the one who waters have one purpose, and they will each be rewarded according to their own labor. For we are co-workers in God's service" (1 Cor 3:8-9).

TUNE THEIR HEARTS TO SING HIS PRAISE

A life properly tuned to God resounds these truths. Teens need to understand that we are intended, responsible, accountable, and together with one another. The quest for identity need not be a solitary journey. It need not be a matter of discovering "what works for me." Instead, the quest for identity becomes a journey with other Christians to find out how we can share in God's rule, love him, and love others with the capacities and within the spheres of influence he has given to each of us.

Teens need to know what a life tuned to God looks like. Give them examples from Scripture and from life. Point to the people who anchor their identity in Christ and exercise responsible stewardship in their spheres of influence.

Help them see themselves in the biblical story and find themselves implicated by it. Rehearse the truth of the gospel and of our union with Christ. Teens live in a world in which it is increasingly difficult to hear the A 440. Give them the pitch again, again, and again.

REFLECTION QUESTIONS

1. In what ways do you see your students trying on different personas? What struggles do they encounter as they seek to understand who they are and what life is all about?
2. Who in your local context anchors their identity in Christ well? How can you invite your students to learn from and imitate these people?
3. How can you continue to grow in your understanding of what it means to find your identity in Christ? How will you share your learning with your students?

———

Meryl Herr is an adjunct professor at Trinity Evangelical Divinity School and Cornerstone University. Her research focuses on young adults' faith-work integration. She lives in Grand Rapids, Michigan, with her husband and two sons.

Youth Pastor as Liturgist

BY CHRIS NEAL

> "We are becoming who we will be forever."
> *Dallas Willard*

I had the privilege of serving as a youth and family ministries pastor in the local church for 12 years. During those years I partnered with many gifted, passionate, and committed leaders who joined me in the work of shepherding students toward Christ as they navigated the complexities of adolescence in an increasingly complex world. We worked hard to faithfully and effectively invite them to be "transformed by the renewing of [their] mind" rather than "conform[ing] to the pattern of this world," as Paul exhorted in Romans 12:2. Yet in terms of depth of influence, it seemed as though our youth ministry lagged significantly behind family systems, peer groups, school culture, extracurricular activities, and social media.

In our city, one of many cities in the sprawling Los Angeles Metropolitan area, there is a large waterpark. It is filled with waterslides, lazy rivers, inflatable raft rides, and a large wave pool. The wave pool is an Olympic-sized pool with a shallow end on one side, a 12-foot deep end on the other, and a buoyed rope separating the two. Built into the side wall in the deep end is a powerful machine designed to form waves and send them rippling across the pool.

A few years ago, while evaluating the impact our youth ministry was having on the spiritual formation of our students, this image of the wave pool came to mind. As I sat with this image, I began to think of the waves serving as a metaphor for our students, and I imagined myself swimming in the deep end along with my team of volunteers. As the wave machine powerfully formed the next wave, my volunteers and I would use all that was at our disposal to try and reshape the waves — hands, feet, foam boards, whatever. We saw clear evidence that our efforts in partnership with, and empowered by the Holy Spirit, were making some difference at changing the shape and direction of some waves, but we also wrestled with the questions, "Is it enough? Is there a better way? Is there a more impactful way of addressing the powerfully formative effects of the wave machine?" As systems theory wisdom suggests — organizations are designed for the results they are currently receiving.

So what are the "results" that the social systems shaping our young people are getting? Jeffrey Arnett argues that people are taking much longer to mature into adulthood.[57] Christian Smith observed how our family and religious systems have primarily shaped our young people to be Moralistic Therapeutic Deists, believing God wants us to be generally good people, but besides serving as an occasional cosmic therapist, God is fundamentally uninvolved and irrelevant with most of life.[58] Chap Clark and Patricia Hersch explain how youth feel abandoned by almost every adult and institution originally designed to support them.[59] And yet, as youth workers we desperately want so much more for our young people. We are passionate to see our young people mature into adulthood at a younger age, more deeply committed to Christ, and equipped with a vision for participating in God's mission in all of life. So how do we begin rethinking our systems in order to see different results? I believe we can learn a lot from James K.A. Smith's work on cultural liturgies.

WHAT ARE CULTURAL LITURGIES?

Before we can unpack this idea of cultural liturgies, we must first begin by understanding liturgy. In my experience of pastoral youth ministry, when people used the term liturgy or the phrase liturgical elements, they were referring to the various elements of a worship service (e.g., praise and worship through music, preaching and teaching, prayer, testimonies, confessions, communion, announcements, etc.). However, the idea of liturgy was somewhat foreign to me, as I often served in churches that could be described as "low church" or having "low liturgy." That is to say that the various liturgical elements of our service were less structured and somewhat more spontaneous than churches with "high liturgy." Prayers were prayed in the moment rather than being scripted prior to the service. The congregation was called to worship by the worship band beginning to play music rather than by the pastor processing down the aisle formally calling everyone to worship. Consequently, this notion of thinking liturgically was fairly new to me despite having grown up in the local church.

The English word "liturgy" is derived from the Greek word, *leitourgia*, which is formed from the combination of the Greek words, *leos*, meaning "people," and *ergon*, meaning "work." The word literally means "the work of the people," and originally was used to refer to all public work. However, throughout church history, the English term began to be used more narrowly to refer to church services, the Eucharist, or the written documents that ordered the church service.[60]We engage these liturgical elements when we gather in worship, believing we are being spiritually formed in Christ. These are sacred actions, practices, and rituals we participate in with the belief, hope, and desire that they help us as a community be transformed toward Christlikeness. As a corollary to Richard Foster's definition of spiritual disciplines, liturgical elements are actions we take that allow God to do what only God can do (i.e., transform us).[61] They are communal worship practices that form us.

Smith invites readers to expand their understanding of liturgy and consider the cultural liturgies that we participate in everyday. Smith defines cultural liturgies as the daily rituals and practices that shape our habits and, consequently, our loves, affections, desires, and hungers. These liturgies contain a *telos*, a story of the ultimate end or purpose of life. In some ways, Smith invites us to recapture the original scope of the word liturgy (all public work) while retaining the formational vision of what the word came to mean. In other words, the language and framework of cultural liturgies helps us recognize the formative effects of the practices, habits, and rituals we participate in everyday.

In his book, *Desiring the Kingdom*, Smith describes the liturgy of the mall, inviting us to recognize this activity as a liturgical practice that is shaping our beliefs and, even more powerfully, our affections or desires. The liturgy of the mall contains various stories of the good life. Embedded in the advertisements, pictures, displays, and products are implicit messages about what we should love as ultimate because in them is access to the good life. He makes the case that simply by shopping at the mall, and participating in the liturgy of the mall, it will potentially malform us toward materialism.[62] "In short, we unconsciously learn to love rival kingdoms because we don't realize we're participating in rival liturgies."[63]

LEARNING TO THINK LITURGICALLY ABOUT
MIDDLE AND HIGH SCHOOL

Let's return for a moment to the wave machine, our opening metaphor for the primary social systems that are shaping our young people (i.e., family, school, friends, social media). What would it look like to begin thinking liturgically about these systems? How are the daily rhythms, rituals, practices of high school forming our students? What is the *telos* of each of these liturgies? What can we discern is the ultimate end or purpose of life based on our family calendar? What does social media invite young people to love as ultimate? While I hope one day to be able to more exhaustively answer these questions, for our purposes here I will simply focus on the last one.

Let's explore for a moment the liturgy of Instagram and consider how it might be forming our students. What is the ultimate end, goal, or telos of life according to Instagram? I think there are actually several, but I will only name a few, focusing primarily on the ones I believe are most malforming our students. First, more followers means more worth. Second, fame is worth any price — death-defying risks, foolish or "ridiculous" behavior, or even exposing your body. Third, life is best spent in leisure while col-

...the language and framework of cultural liturgies helps us recognize the formative effects of the *practices, habits, and rituals* we participate in everyday."

lecting as many experiences as possible from around the world. These are not messages that are explicitly stated, nor propaganda that is intentionally marketed to people. These are the messages we inherit naturally by viewing thousands of pictures and videos. Videos of someone who has more than one million followers for posting videos of them dangling by one hand from skyscrapers. Pictures of people who retired young with plenty of wealth to constantly travel the world. Pictures of people living off of sponsorships because they regularly post pictures of their body they meticulously shaped through diet and exercise.

I would imagine, as our students scroll through their feed, there are many strong emotions they might feel. As they see photos of celebrities living the culturally defined "good life," they may experience envy and jealousy. As they see photos with thousands or even millions of likes, they may feel inferior or even invisible with their 16 likes. As they see curated pictures of friends hanging out without them, they may feel angry, lonely, or isolated. Over time, as our students (and adults) participate in this liturgy on a regular basis, they will possibly be formed by this cultural liturgy, growing more lonely, jealous, and angry.

We, the Youth Leadership Initiative at Azusa Pacific University, produced a monograph (a single-subject book) on the rise of anxiety, depression, and self-harm among adolescents. In the monograph we do not research the causes of this rise, but simply focus on reporting the current stats while helping youth workers begin to develop best practices to support students.[64] However, part of me wonders if there is a link between the cultural liturgies of social media and the rise of adolescent anxiety and depression. Does social media enable students to over consume culturally defined stories of the "good life" while simultaneously sending the message that their life does not measure up? Is this a contributing factor to the rise of anxiety and depression among adolescents?

I believe we need to intentionally cultivate, with the help of the

Holy Spirit, a faith in our students that equips them to face these cultural liturgies and still be conformed to the image of Christ and not the image of our world.

REIMAGINING CHRISTIAN FORMATION

Based on observation, it would seem that much of our modern discipleship practices, at least in the West, are often rooted in a Cartesian understanding of what it means to be human, placing the intellect and right beliefs at the forefront of discipleship and spiritual formation. René Descartes was the 17th century French philosopher who is most popularly known for saying "I think, therefore I am." Descartes believed the fundamental nature of humans was as "thinking things."

Our bodies are more or less transportation mechanisms for our brains, which are the seat of reason and the fundamental aspect of what it means to be human. Consequently, people are simply thinking things; nothing more than "brains-on-a-stick."[65]

Smith disagrees with this anthropology, this vision of what it means to be human, and raises some powerful and poignant questions:

> What if, instead of starting from the assumption that human beings are thinking things, we started from the conviction that human beings are first and foremost lovers? What if you are defined not by what you know but by what you desire? What if the center and seat of the human person is found not in the heady regions of the intellect but in the gut-level regions of the heart? How would that change our approach to discipleship and Christian formation?[66]

Smith roots these questions and his convictions in what he observes in Jesus' words and ministry. "Jesus doesn't encoun-

I believe we need — cultivate, with the a faith in our students face these cultural conformed to the and not the

→ to intentionally
help of the Holy Spirit,
that equips them to
liturgies and still be
image of Christ
image of our world.

CHRIS NEAL

ter Matthew and John — or you and me — and ask, 'What do you know?' He doesn't even ask, 'What do you believe?' He asks, 'What do you want?'"[67]

While we see in Paul's words in Romans 12:2 that we are "transformed by the renewing of our minds," does this mean Paul agrees with Descartes that we simply need to impart the right information and then right actions will naturally flow? I do not think so. I believe Paul is rooted in a more holistic view of the human person. As we see in Jesus' words in the Great Commandment of Luke 10:27 (NIV), "Love the Lord your God with all your heart and with all your soul and with all your strength and with all your mind." Within Romans 12:1-2, we also see more holistic language. We are to "offer [our] bodies as a living sacrifice," which is our "true and proper worship," and we are to be "transformed by the renewing of our minds." This is not a Cartesian picture of right thinking equaling right action. There is a dynamic and integrated relationship between right beliefs (orthodoxy), right actions (orthopraxy), and right love and desires (orthopathy).

PERSONAL AND CORPORATE CHRISTIAN FORMATION IN LIGHT OF CULTURAL LITURGIES

James Smith reframes worship and Christian formation as counter cultural rehabituation of our loves.[68] If it is true that cultural liturgies are malforming our loves through our daily rituals and practices, then our discipleship practices must specifically be designed to reshape our loves so we only love God as ultimate and so we grow in loving what God loves. How do we do this? While I believe there is much untapped potential for how the idea of cultural liturgies can help us reimagine more faithful and formative discipleship practices, I will simply share three ideas.

First, invite students to take a liturgical audit, prayerfully examining who they are becoming. This will help students grow in self-awareness which will help them recognize how they are changing, while also preparing them to recognize rival liturgies while they are participating in them. Smith recommends a set of questions for taking a liturgical audit:

- What are the things you do that can shape you?
- What are the secular liturgies in your life?
- What vision of the good life is carried in those liturgies?
- What Story is embedded in those cultural practices?
- What kind of person do they want you to become?
- To what kingdom are these rituals aimed?
- What does this cultural institution want you to love?[69]

This is a good list, though I would add a few more to help translate this thinking into a youth ministry context:

- As you think of the different authority figures in your life (e.g., parents, teachers, coaches, pastors, etc.), what is their story of the good life?
- As you think about your closest friends, what is their story of the good life?
- As you reflect on your time spent on social media, what are the top three emotions you experience? How would you say that your time on social media is affecting or changing you as a person? What stories of the good life on social media are you most drawn to? What is the primary thing you would say that you want or desire after spending time on social media?

Second, equip our students with spiritual disciplines that enable them to access the transformative power of Christ amidst the cultural liturgies shaping them. At our church, we encourage our community to write and memorize a simple prayer for particular situations that malform us. Each simple prayer includes three elements: An honest confession of reality; A Christocentric reframing of reality; and a request for God's help. For example, if a student regularly struggles with jealousy after spending time on Instagram, their simple prayer might be, "God I am jealous because I want the lives my friends have, but I am your masterpiece created in Christ Jesus to do good works. Help me want the life you have for me."

Third, reimagine the liturgy of our youth services to not simply inform students about who God is and what God desires, but to actually help our students love God as ultimate and love what he loves. How can we design our worship gatherings to not simply inform students about God, but actually help reform them to love what God loves? Over the years in different seasons, I and other youth workers near me have used the format of *Head, Hands, Heart*, which is a concept that made its way into the youth ministry world from the educational world.[70] I believe this concept integrates well to a holistic approach to corporate learning environments.

What are we offering for their head, to expand their thinking, to develop their beliefs, and cultivate orthodoxy? How are we equipping their hands, preparing them to live and act faithfully, helping them to live orthopraxy? Finally, how are we inspiring their heart, shaping their loves, and cultivating orthopathy? While I affirm this holistic model, I believe what we have seen so far is that it can be easy to only focus on head and hands while cultural liturgies go straight to the heart, and in order to address cultural liturgies we need to give special attention to how we are addressing the heart of our students.

DISCUSSION QUESTIONS:

1. What are the primary cultural liturgies shaping your students?
2. In each of those liturgies, what is the story of the good life being conveyed to your students?

3. As you reflect on the times when your church or ministry gathers young people, how could that time more faithfully and formatively help students love God as ultimate and learn to love what God loves?

―――

Chris Neal is director of the Youth Leadership Initiative in the Center for Vocational Ministry at Azusa Pacific University, serves as a City Network Leader for Made to Flourish in Los Angeles, and is a Ph.D. student at Fuller Seminary. He is a native of Los Angeles where he currently lives with his wife and three daughters.

Youth Pastor as Cultural Facilitator

BY YULEE LEE

> "Life's most persistent and urgent question is,
> What are you doing for others?" *Martin Luther King, Jr.*

Growing up Asian-American in Salt Lake City, Utah, was not easy. During my walk home from school, I would often be followed by kids who chanted racist slurs or asked if I knew Bruce Lee.[71] Every week, I came home angry and spent many hours imagining plans of revenge. With hard-working immigrant parents, I didn't have anyone at home who could help me process my experiences. We attended a local Korean-American church, but I felt ashamed and insecure to voice my pain. It was during this season of life when I was convicted to fight for change on behalf of others who were vulnerable and marginalized.

Fast-forward to high school, where my battles were expressed through protests on my local government's steps, or a fiercely angry call to the manager of Applebee's due to the racism I experienced because I was asked to wait too long to be seated. There's nothing wrong with my expressions of frustration, but I had enough young instinct to know my fight for others shouldn't be primarily driven by unprocessed pain that bulldozed over some people in order to make way for others. This is why I think the question Martin Luther King, Jr. asks above becomes so persistent and urgent — as human beings, even with good intentions, we can deceive ourselves to think we are actually doing something for others when, in fact, we might be perpetuating the violence we're working to prevent. King Jr.'s question confronts us as individuals, collectives, and churches and keeps us reflectively accountable to our Christian responsibility to love others like ourselves, which is an increasingly difficult endeavor in the world today.

In their book *Growing Young,* Powell, Mulder, and Griffin reveal that churches experience challenges when it comes to helping youth navigate the complexities of culture.[72] This is not surprising given the rapid rate of change in our increasingly globalized world.[73] Youth pastors are often caught in the intersection of young people and their interaction with culture change. Within this intersection, youth pastors are in unique positions of influence as cultural facilitators – wise guides who create space, provide support, and challenge young people to follow Jesus holistically in their engagement of the world. As cultural facilitators, youth pastors have opportunity to steward the integration of young people's love for God and love for neighbor in ways that can fruitfully contribute to the common good as culture makers.[74] Discipling youth toward an holistic engagement for the common good can be a valuable gift to a generation of young people who are passionate and eager to make social change.[75]

Why is it important for youth pastors to cultivate culture makers? Because we've been designed and equipped to be culture makers — co-creators with God to shape the world as he intended (Gen 1:26-28). Dating back to Adam and Eve, God equips his people for meaningful work that adds value to the world. God gave

Adam and Eve physical work (gardening in Genesis 2:15) and cultural work (naming animals in Genesis 2:19-20). As image-bearers of God, youth are designed with a divine purpose to extend the creative work of God and to reflect God in the work they do. This also means God created youth to live in community and relationship with others. Youth pastors need to recognize how our increasingly global and culturally complex world influences youth like never before, and their cultural context shapes who they are, thereby making them cultural experts in their own right.[76] When we recognize youth contribute a unique lens and skill set, we can empower them to be redemptive culture makers.

Our churches need youth pastors who can put on the hat of cultural facilitator. Putting on this hat requires youth workers to

Within this intersection, youth pastors are in unique positions of influence as *cultural facilitators* – wise guides who *create space*, *provide support*, and *challenge young people* to follow Jesus holistically in their engagement of the world.

push themselves to be global citizens and not to be complacent in a mono-ethnic or ethnic majority — a push to grow as ministers of the gospel who are acutely aware of cultural shifts for the sake of the next generation. The Gen Z's who are currently in our youth ministries[77] have the world as their classroom through technology. They are likely growing up much more diverse than their parents and youth workers. However, in many instances, the established church is having a hard time keeping up with cultural change. What can we do to serve young people today? We can listen to the voices of young people to help us see the culture more clearly and speak its language. It's time our churches give full membership to young culture makers as part of the body of Christ and family of God.

This chapter does not attempt to give you neat, clear answers to share with your church or youth group. There is no cut-and-paste method or toolkit that will be provided. Rather, the purpose of this chapter is to challenge youth pastors to either reframe and/or fully embrace their role as cultural facilitators who have a critical opportunity to develop and launch a new generation of culture makers. I hope this chapter challenges us to integrate our thinking about our faith so we can grow more aware of our own convictions and grow in wisdom to live for the common good.

YOUTH AS CULTURE MAKERS

My senior high school days were mostly spent building a well-rounded portfolio of unique activities and a 4.2 grade point average. As an Asian-American youth with immigrant parents, academic superiority was especially important: Getting straight As, staying on National Honors Society, and participating in extracurricular activities — all culminating in acceptance to a college (preferably an Ivy League that all other Asians knew about), leading to a job that would let me contribute to the world as a responsible citizen. All the while, as an Asian-American youth raised in a predominantly white community, I also felt an inner angst to make the world a better place than the one I experienced from the voiceless margins.

After participating in countless protests or yelling matches with school bullies that did not result in change, I thought the key to world change was more education and a good job. Of course, God does use education and jobs to increase our spheres of influence. What I did not realize in my youth, however, is that God is already at work changing the world around me, and as God's beloved I could participate with him to influence and contribute to his economy.

Your youth group is filled with students just like me — youth who are unaware of their God-given agency to partner with him in his redemptive plan for the world in their season of life and within their given contexts. Rather than being driven by the gospel, often catalyzed by a Christocentric community of belonging, youth turn to social media with friendship-driven or interest-driven hopes.[78] Churches do a disservice to youth when they neglect to directly communicate the divine significance youth hold, and create a community that provides space and guidance for them to be culture makers in our world. We continue to marginalize youth within our churches by not listening to their voices, judging their unique perspectives, and disrespecting their dignity and agency to lead us (I have been guilty of this too). What if our youth groups could be spaces that cultivate gospel-driven youth who not only intentionally and courageously engage their world, but fully embrace their role in creating new culture?

This is possible when youth pastors believe youth are culture makers in the name of Jesus. Crystal Kirgiss writes, "adolescents have much to teach us and show us about his character."[79] When we invite the next generation as prophetic voices that can influence and shape culture, we facilitate an experience that is spiritually formative for youth, ourselves, and our churches. When we recognize youth as culture makers, we recognize "God's original

When we recognize youth contribute a *unique lens* and skill set,

we can empower
them to be
redemptive
culture makers.

YULEE LEE

Churches do a disservice to youth when they neglect to *directly communicate* the divine significance youth hold, and *create a community* that provides space and guidance for them to be culture makers in our world.

job description for mankind that they have a role in partnering with God to fill the earth — creating culture that affirms his values of goodness, truth, and beauty."[80] It makes sense why youth already create new cultural goods everyday like new languages, handshakes, or dance moves. It makes sense why youth create new clubs in their schools or participate in national school walkouts in protest of gun violence. They are made in the image of a Creator who calls us to steward a responsibility to create and cultivate culture on earth (Gen1-2). This is where your role as cultural facilitator can make a difference in influencing a generation of redemptive change agents that help advance the kingdom of God.

CULTIVATING CHRISTLIKE CARE IN YOUNG ADULTS
One way youth pastors can disciple young culture makers is to cultivate care in the lives of youth. Cultivating care can be a chal-

lenge, however, when so much in the world competes for their attention, with much of after-school activity involving some use of technology.[81] Because youth are immersed in technology, they come to us every Sunday morning with significant knowledge of world events and cultural insight. In conversations with youth, I realized how they already care about specific people, craft specific plans for their week, and make decisions based on specific preferences that give them a sense of identity and belonging. Isn't this true of older people, too? Human beings usually want to talk about and make plans and decisions around what we care about. When was the last time you sat with a young person and listened empathically about who or what is on her mind and why? These conversations are critical because they provide an opportunity to learn what young people naturally care about. When you discover what motivates your youth to care, you can create the conditions to cultivate Christlike care in ways that are spiritually formational.

The framework for cultivating Christlike care that is compassionate begins under the umbrella of God's love for humanity where he relates to his creation with compassion (Matt 9:36).[82] The word *compassion* has Hebrew and Aramaic roots meaning "inward parts, what the Old King James version used to call *bowels of mercy*. It comes from the same source as the word *womb*."[83] Compassion's deeper meaning implies not only that it emerges from the core of who we are but it also serves as an incubator for new life and growth. This action-oriented characteristic of compassion is what distinguishes it from pity. In fact, "*pity* denotes the feeling of empathetic identification with the sufferer, and *compassion* refers to the feeling accompanied by action."[84]

As we guide youth to express their care in ways that reflect biblical compassion, we can point them to Jesus' action-oriented embodiment of compassionate care. We cannot possibly cover all the ways in which Jesus shows compassion in this field guide, but I will share two interrelated examples from the life of Jesus that are necessary yet increasingly challenging in our busy, high-tech, fear-driven Western culture.

First, Jesus initiates conversations with others and takes time to understand who they are. Without knowing someone, how can we truly care? We see this in his interaction with the Samaritan woman in John 4:7-42. During a time when Jews were not supposed to interact with Samaritans, Jesus chose to build the bridge between himself and someone who was not part of the in-crowd. He listened to her story, saw who she was, and affirmed her contribution to the conversation. The interaction transformed her life as well as many other Samaritans who believed in Jesus due to this relational testimony. As youth seek to "care" for others, youth pastors have an opportunity to cultivate a kind of care that is rooted in real relationships and compassionate care. Relationships with people who are different from us are critical to knowing how to care well.

Second, Jesus specifically cares for the most vulnerable and marginalized people of our world. The liberation perspective suggests that by selecting a ministry to the socially cast out, and being biased against the powers and oppressive systems of his day, Jesus was, in fact, embracing others *because* of their social standing.[85] Caring for the vulnerable and marginalized does not mean "liking" a tweet or Facebook post about them. Caring for the vulnerable and marginalized means going into their contexts, learning from them, and partnering with them to make the world a better place. For example, a good place to start is to ask these two questions, "Who and Where are the most vulnerable in our cities and neighborhoods?" "In what ways have they been marginalized (socially, economically, educationally, etc.)?" This is difficult and uncomfortable, but the ministry of Christ to all human beings is the work that young people can continue in the world through the empowerment of the Holy Spirit.

Discipling youth to grow in compassionate care through genuine relationships with others does not necessarily mean you encourage youth to create a nonprofit to serve the homeless. Rather, it is the process of facilitating their discovery of redemptive purpose, meaning, and beauty in the everyday ordinary work that takes place all around them.[86] The hope is that youth workers can provide opportunities to learn from diverse people and communities, exposing their youth to artisans, businesses, and entrepreneurs who contribute value socially, economically, and politically for the common good. Processing such experiences through reflective dialogue can be transformative for young people. Further, these reflective conversations can generate collective action from this generation of culture makers.

CREATING A COMMUNITY THAT EMPOWERS YOUNG ADULTS

How do we create environments where youth can dream their own ways of culture making as well as provide the support and structure they need to engage their ideas? How can we integrate youth and culture making opportunities so young people can learn, reflect, and grow from the process? Youth pastors can create the conditions for a youth group culture where young people can co-create and make meaningful contributions to the common good. As a cultural facilitator, youth pastors can build discipleship entry points to shepherd young people as global kingdom citizens who are not only aware of, but can also enter into the social, economic, and political currents of our day. One entry point can be through the power of a dialogical community where listening, respecting, suspending judgment, and voicing can both be a model and container for young people to talk, think, and act together. The dialogical community is a place that allows others to speak into, sharpen, dream about, and perhaps even challenge ideas about affecting change with love and humility. In its essence, the dialogical community calls forth the body of Christ to practice what we preach.

How can youth workers create an environment where a diverse group of young people can engage in a kind of conversation that deepens relationships by unearthing assumptions and challenging youth to learn from *and* with one another? This is where the process and art of dialogue comes in. It is a misunderstood and rare form of communication, especially in churches, but even more so in youth groups. But, that's what makes its potential all the more exciting. What is dialogue? Dialogue is a process of communication that encourages people to come together as equals to think, reflect and create as a collective whole. It is "a conversation with a center, not sides."[87]

The beauty and mystery of dialogue is that it creates spaces for young people to gather — just as they are — and to engage, as equals, with their peers and their leaders to seek a greater understanding not only of who they are as individuals and the assumptions they carry, but to gain a more profound understanding of their neighbor[88] at the same time. Any thought or idea can be explored. Sometimes, deep healing occurs. Youth may experience fresh connection with others and begin to see and understand potential "enemies" as co-creators of a new, more meaningful future.

Dialogue is important in youth groups because of its potential to catalyze inward transformation, which is a smart place to begin the journey of influencing external change. Dialogue is a process that requires practice and experience so that people can continue to grow the capacity for dialogue and eventually come to embody dialogic practice. This applies to both youth workers as facilitators and young people as participants. I cannot underscore enough the point that successful execution of dialogue requires practice and experience. It is similar to growing our capacity for spiritual disciplines like fasting or silence and solitude. The more you try to engage youth in dialogue, the more you will increase the capacity for dialogic practice. It's hard work, but you will be cultivating a culture of learning for young people that holds potential to create relational cohesion and collective empowerment, which is key to bridging diverse young culture makers.

Discipling youth to grow in *compassionate care* through genuine relationships with others does not necessarily mean you encourage youth to create a nonprofit to serve the homeless. Rather, it is the process of facilitating their discovery of *redemptive purpose*, *meaning*, and *beauty* in the everyday ordinary work that takes place all around them.

HOW CAN I PRACTICE DIALOGUE IN MY YOUTH MINISTRY?

How do you execute dialogic practice with young people? You can facilitate dialogue in a variety of ways, but in the context of youth ministry, I have found dialogue can be fruitful when it stems from experience. If you know your youth well, you can draw out their experiences. If that makes you nervous, you can engage them in dialogue about a shared experience, perhaps serving your local community or even a shared emotional experience. Whichever catalyst you choose, here are some practical steps to help get you started.

1. Set aside 30 minutes for the first dialogue experience. You can increase the time allotment as your group grows in dialogic capacity.

2. Gather your young people together. If this is your first time convening a dialogue experience, I recommend starting with a group of 12 young people, but feel free to use your discernment based on your own context.

3. Have everyone sit in a big circle. The circle is critical. No tables needed.

4. Once everyone is gathered, communicate what will happen. Explain how you will facilitate a different kind of conversation called dialogue. Explain that there is no real curriculum for their time together and you want to hear what's on their minds and hearts. Explain that to do this well, we will need to remember the four ingredients of dialogue (listening, respecting, suspending judgment, voicing)[89] — even write those on a whiteboard or some other big sheet of paper to act as a visual reminder.

5. Pray with your young people as a way to welcome the Holy Spirit into your dialogue space.

6. Name the shared experience your group will be talking about out loud and write a question or statement on the whiteboard that will serve as a prompt regarding the dialogue topic.

7. Remind them they can share whatever is on their minds or hearts about the topic.

8. At this point, your role as the facilitator becomes crucial. Let the conversation build and be patient. There will be moments of silence, which is normal and good.

There might be conflict, which is normal. Let them sit in the disorientation of different perspectives. Use your discernment to know when and how to move the conversation along by remembering the focal point but perhaps contributing a story or different angle. To guide the process, contribute your voice as an equal, and try not to enter into teaching mode.

9. Give space for youth to develop their own action points and guide them through execution, which will be messy and lovely all together. Ask them what they can do together about what they now know?

10. At the end of your time together, thank everyone for their contribution to the dialogue and close in prayer.

11. Make sure you, as a youth worker, reflect on the process by yourself and with your leadership. A lot of interesting observations and data will surface that will help inform your spiritual formation goals going forward.

Seek to embed dialogic practice by iterating conversation upon conversation, and see how deep and wide your youth can take you on the journey of culture making.

———

Yulee Lee is the director of the Office of Christian Outreach at Wheaton College. She's also finishing her Ph.D. in Educational Studies at Trinity Evangelical Divinity School. Yulee and her family reside in Buffalo Grove, Illinois.

Conclusion

BY AMBER STEELE

Youth pastors wear many hats, even more than the ones that have been discussed here in this field guide. As a youth pastor, you play a vital role in equipping students with a deep understanding of the integration of faith and work. The good news is this can be done (and should be done) through the roles you already play.

As theologians or teachers of God, youth pastors disciple students in all areas of their lives and equip them to embody their faith wherever they find themselves during the week (all seven days). Our role is to teach students how their secondary callings (sons/daughters, siblings, students, athletes, workers) are in response to God's primary calling. A rich theology of faith and work must be taught, and it is critical that it is connected with the grand story of Scripture. God's grand mission in the world is directly connected with how we spend our days. We need to be master storytellers of the four-chapter gospel, beginning in Genesis and ending in Revelation: creation, fall, redemption, and consummation. It is vital our students understand how they spend their time at school, work, and everywhere else matters for the kingdom of God.

As guidance counselors, youth pastors help students bring a robust sense of calling to their education. We must emphasize the importance of school being the ordinary, secondary calling for students. It is their workplace. This emphasis can be achieved with three areas of focus: involvement, relationships, and academics. We can help them connect to something bigger than themselves, to God's big story. We must teach about the dangers of isolation and the importance of asking for help when needed. Lastly, we must emphasize how education is more than just the transfer of information; it is a formational project. Some practical ways to walk alongside our students as they begin to see school as one of their secondary callings include celebrating school instead of speaking negatively about it, spending time in school with your students, and teaching about school as work.

As psychologists, youth pastors help students navigate the journey of identity development and encourage them to find their fundamental identity in Christ. The Christian's quest for identity begins with being in-tune with God. A life properly tuned to God resounds four truths. We are intended by God and created for a purpose so we can partner with God in his redemptive mission in the world. We are responsible; God shared his rule with us and calls us to stewardship of his rule within our spheres of influence. We are accountable; God expects us to steward our time, talent and treasures well. We are together; we are coworkers in God's service. We must walk alongside our students and equip and encourage them as they tune their hearts to sing his praise and see themselves in the biblical story.

As liturgists, youth pastors help guide students to love what God loves. Cultural liturgies are the daily activities and practices that shape our habits and consequently our loves, affections, and desires. These rituals we participate in everyday are formative and tell a story of the ultimate purpose of life. We must learn to think liturgically about middle and high school life. How might the liturgy of things like social media be forming our students? They need to be equipped to face these cultural liturgies and still be conformed to the image of Christ. To do this, we need to reimagine Christian formation and focus on a more holistic view of the human person: heart, soul, strength, and mind. We can start with inviting students to take a liturgical audit, then equip them with practices that enable them to access the transformative power of Christ amidst the cultural liturgies shaping them. Lastly, reimagine our youth ministries in a way that will help our students to actually love God above everything else.

As cultural facilitators, youth pastors are wise guides who create space, provide support, and challenge students to follow Jesus holistically in their engagement of the world. We have the amazing opportunity to steward the integration of student's love for God and love for neighbor in ways that can fruitfully contribute to the common good. In order to do this well, we must increase our cultural awareness and push ourselves to be global citizens. We need to become more aware of our own convictions and be more wise, intentional, and courageous enough to live them out for the common good. We must listen to the voices of young people. Jesus is inviting our students into his ministry of world redemption. As we disciple these young culture makers, we should cultivate care in their lives and also create a community that empowers them (support and structure). The process of dialogue can play a key role in achieving these goals as it creates a culture of learning that has the potential to bring about relational cohesion and collective empowerment.

These are just five of the many hats you wear as youth pastors, but you can see the scope is deep and wide for the faith and work conversation. We hope this field guide has been a great introduction for you and helps you reimagine many aspects of your ministry to students. Can you imagine the impact this way of viewing our work might have on our students both now and in the future? What steps will you take today to integrate these practices into your youth ministry and equip your students with a rich theology of faith and work? Our team is praying for you as you shepherd and equip your students and partner with God in your work as a youth pastor.

———

Amber Steele is the Director of Children, Youth and Family Ministries at Christ Community Church of the South Hills in Pittsburgh, Pennsylvania. Amber and her husband, Greg, have four children: Caleb, Megan, Micah and Caroline.

Appendix:
Helping Students
Discern Future Calling

Hopefully we have made a compelling case that the schooling of the middle and high school students in our youth groups ought to be viewed as one of their secondary callings, an incredible opportunity for them to serve God with devotion and serve their fellows students in love.

However, while we need to remain lifelong *learners*, no one does (or even should) remain a lifelong student. Therefore, we can, as youth pastors, serve our students well by beginning a conversation about *future* work and the importance of discerning future, secondary callings.

This is, of course, a recent conversation. Throughout most of history, the idea of multiple vocational options, of choice in the conversation about calling, would have been completely foreign. Your dad was the neighborhood blacksmith? Welcome to the world of blacksmithing! Even today, across our broad and diverse globe, many people do not experience the opportunity of having choices many students in our youth groups experience.

Acknowledging this reality is important, but it does not mean it is inappropriate to help our students navigate the choices they do face. In fact, we would submit that would be inappropriate to let them leave our youth groups *without* this conversation. Too many students don't begin to think about this soon enough, and many others enter into the conversation with the wrong inputs. As youth pastors, we need to be at the table, helping our students think biblically about their futures, and about what God is preparing them for and calling them into.

We also need to acknowledge the undue influence higher education wielded the last 125 years upon secondary education. In *The Rise and Fall of the American Teenager*, Thomas Hines argues that while the original goal of high school was to prepare adolescents for life, this has shifted to preparing students for entrance into college. He explains that while preparing adolescents for life is a worthy goal, it takes literally a lifetime to assess your effectiveness. Yet a high college admissions rate is an immediate indicator of success for a school. Hine later explains why he disagrees with this approach:

> Yet there has always been a problem with such a college-centered approach. In the nineteenth century, the majority of high school students didn't even graduate. Today the great majority do, but it's still not clear that pointing everyone toward college is the best way to help each students develop his or her particular talents and prepare to make a living.[90]

We reject the notion that every high school student must attend college. Many should, but others should consider a career in the military or learn the value of gaining trade skills that help society in invaluable ways.

Youth pastors can come alongside upperclassmen as they discern next steps. Ask diagnostic questions: What are you curious about? What comes naturally to you that others seem to struggle with? What threads of interest have been most consistent in your life? Then, speak the truth of what you see in your student and offer to pray with them.

Think bigger, too, and practically. What if you took a page out of any good guidance counselor's playbook and scheduled a "what's coming after high school?" meeting with the juniors in your youth group and their parents? Not to provide answers, but to have a place to ask questions, give guidance, and pray together.

Are there students in your youth group that are navigating these questions without parents, or without engaged parents? How could you creatively stand in that gap? Perhaps you could offer to take them on college/trade school visits, or help them with scholarship applications. For all of your students, make it known you would be honored to serve as a reference for them as they apply to what's next — whether that be school or a job in the workforce.

Once the students in your group graduate and transition, stick with them. Write them notes encouraging them to be faithful and fruitful in this new chapter. If you can, visit them in their new station as they live out a new, secondary calling.

With students of all ages, ask what they want to do when they finish high school, a twist on the "what do you want to be when you grow up?" classic. You might be tempted to think that middle or high school students have outgrown this question, but you'd be surprised how much they are still thinking about this.

When I (Paul) asked this question in my youth group during a message on faith and work integration, it gave me the opportunity to affirm the vital vocation of stay-at-home parents, as one middle school girl said she wanted to be a mom. "That's awesome, Kira!" I replied, "Don't let anyone talk you out of that if God is calling you to it." Those are the moments we're looking for in this conversation, and they often aren't as far away as we think.

Acknowledgments

Someone said that "teamwork makes the dream work." This person is certainly right. I invited a team of talented and passionate writers to curate content that introduces youth ministers to the faith, work, and economic wisdom conversation. I am thankful for my accomplished A-team of writers: Meryl Herr, Yulee Lee, Nathan Miller, Paul Brandes, and Christopher Neal. These writers have either served as a youth minister, researched youth culture, or currently serve in a church.

Along the way, they submitted outlines of their chapters, and eventually, a fully developed manuscript. At each step of the way, we solicited the voluntary services of a seasoned review board to carefully check the outlines and manuscripts not only for grammar and theological preciseness but for universality, too. We wanted this book to have broad appeal denominationally, ethnically, racially, and socio-economically; a broad appeal so youth ministers in the urban core to the youth minister in the suburbs could benefit from this work. This review board kept us honest and on task.

So, we are thankful for our stellar review board: Amber Steele, Jason Ashimoto, Theo Lai, Michael Mata, Kris Fernhout, Josh Parsons, April Diaz, Zachs Gaiya, Adam Mearse, Suzie Sang, and James King. Special thanks to our managing editor, RuthAnne Irvin, whose editing and organizing acumen was invaluable.

This primer is far better because of their collective experience, generosity, wisdom, insight, and suggestions.

ENDNOTES

1 Bruce Riley Ashford, *Theology and Practice of Mission: God, the Church, and the Nations* (Nashville: B & H Academic, 2011), 6.

2 The youth we serve are included in the "all" reaching maturity and the "whole measure" of Christ's fullness, which is the church in verse 13.

3 We want winsome students who use "gracious and salty speech with outsiders" (Col 4:5-6) and engage in cultural conversations with Christ-like confidence, "shrewd as snakes and as innocent as doves," (Matt 10:16).

4 John R. W. Stott, *Issues Facing Christians Today* (Grand Rapids: Zondervan, 2006), 225.

5 Our vocations within the economy allow us to practice the Great Commandment: "The purpose of vocation is to love and serve one's neighbor...This means that I serve you with my talents, and you serve me with your talents. The result is a divine division of labor in which everyone is constantly giving and receiving in a vast interchange, a unity of diverse people in a social order whose substance and energy is love." Veith, *God at Work*, 39-40.

6 Consider ways to publically honor your students through celebrating cultural "rites of passage," like getting a driver's license, a job (or promotion), school awards, etc. and commissioning them to be the "hands and feet" of Jesus on their sports team, in their clubs, or on their band trip.

7 Kate Harris, "Defining Vocation," *Q Commons*. Address presented at the Q Women and Calling. November, 2013.

8 For example, God called Paul to be an apostle (1 Cor 1:2), called the church in Corinth to be "holy" (1 Cor 1:2) and "peaceful" (1 Cor 7:15), and calls "each person [to] live as a believer in whatever situation the Lord has assigned to them, just as God has called them" (1 Cor 7:17).

9 Os Guinness, *The Call: Finding and Fulfilling the Central Purpose of Your Life* (Nashville: Thomas Nelson, 2003), 47-53.

10 Ibid., 31.

11 The Apostle Peter writes, "Each of you should use whatever gift you have received to serve others, as faithful stewards of God's grace in its various forms. If anyone speaks, they should do so as one who speaks the very words

of God. If anyone serves, they should do so with the strength God provides, so that in all things God may be praised through Jesus Christ. To him be the glory" (1 Pet 4:10).

[12] Dorothy Sayers, *Letters to a Diminished Church: Passionate arguments for the Relevance of Christian Doctrine* (Nashville: Thomas Nelson, 2004), 134-135.

[13] Steven Garber, *Visions of Vocation: Common Grace for the Common Good* (Downers Grove, IL: Intervarsity Press, 2014), 18.

[14] Storytelling is at the heart of what it is to be the Church. When Jesus sent out his apostles, launching the global church, he told them, "You will receive power when the Holy Spirit comes on you; and you will be my witnesses in Jerusalem, and in all Judea and Samaria, and to the ends of the earth" (Acts 1:8). As witnesses, Jesus empowered them to tell his story far and wide. Jesus understood the transformative power of his gospel story. When people hear the Jesus story, accompanied by the power of the Holy Spirit, their eyes open to God's glory and their lives are forever changed. For example, Peter tells the Jesus story at Pentecost in Acts 2 and 3000 people join the Christian church in one day (Acts 2:41). Even earlier, in the Old Testament, the Psalmist explains how every generation must share the story of God to the subsequent generation (Ps 145:4-7).

[15] The Four-Chapter Gospel has also been called "the grand biblical narrative," "the grand story," and a "reformational worldview," since many theologians during the Protestant Reformation rediscovered this biblical teaching on the depth and scope of sin and redemption. Albert M. Wolters, *Creation Regained: Biblical Basics for a Reformational Worldview* (Grand Rapids: Eerdmans, 2005), 1.

[16] Ibid., 11.

[17] Craig Bartholomew and Michael Goheen, *The Drama of Scripture: Finding Our Place in the Biblical Story*, 2nd ed. (Grand Rapids: Baker Academic, 2014), 22.

[18] "This Story, which makes a central claim to history, especially at its most radical point, the resurrection of Jesus from the dead, can be tested; it has proven it can be trusted; and it gives me confidence that the bookends, no less than the book, say something uniquely true about our beginnings, and our ending." Andy Crouch, *Culture Making: Recovering our Creative Calling*

(Downers Grove, IL: InterVarsity Press, 2008), 120.

[19] This term comes from Bill Peale, who mentioned it in a personal conversation on Sunday, Sept. 30, 2018.

[20] "When the name 'work' is given to God's six days of creation, human work is ennobled to the highest conceivable degree, as being the copy of this model." See Franz Delitzsch and Sophia Taylor, *A New Commentary on Genesis* (Eugene, OR: Wipf and Stock Publishers, 2001), 106.

[21] John Mark Comer, *Garden City: Work, Rest, and the Art of Being Human* (Grand Rapids: Zondervan, 2017), 122-123.

[22] Bill Hendricks, *The Person Called You: Why You're Here, Why You Matter & What You Should Do With Your Life* (Chicago: Moody, 2014), 66.

[23] Bartholomew and Goheen, *The Drama of Scripture*, 40.

[24] As the Apostle Paul writes, "Although they claimed to be wise, they became fools and exchanged the glory of the immortal God for images made to look like a mortal human being and birds and animals and reptiles (Rom 1:22-23).

[25] In *The Gospel at Work: How Working for King Jesus Gives Purpose and Meaning to Our Jobs* (Grand Rapids: Zondervan, 2013), Greg Gilbert and Sebastian Traeger explain these two extremes to avoid — we can be *idle* in our work or we can make an *idol* out of our work.

[26] This summary of Haley Gorenson Jacob's thesis could be explained more fully, "In short, what I have argued here in Romans 8:29-30 is that Paul sees that those conformed to the image of the Son are those who, though once participants in the Adamic submission to the powers of sin and death, now participate in the reign of the new Adam over creation. Mankind's position on earth as God's vicegerents to his creation is now restored, though now through the image of the Son of God, who reigns as God's preeminent vicegerent...Those conformed to the image of God's Son participate in the Firstborn Son's sovereign position over creation as adopted members of God's eschatological family and, as such, as a reglorified humanity." Haley Goranson Jacob, *Conformed to the Image of His Son: Reconsidering Paul's Theology of Glory in Romans* (Downers Grove, IL: InterVarsity, 2018), 226-227.

[27] http://www.letterstotheexiles.com

[28] Christopher J. H. Wright, *The Mission of God's People: A Biblical Theology of*

the Church's Mission (Grand Rapids: Zondervan, 2010), 31.

[29] Robert Farrar Capon, *The Supper of the Lamb: A Culinary Reflection* (New York: Modern Library, 2002), 189.

[30] Theologians like George Eldon Ladd have pointed out that although Jesus inaugurated his kingdom at his coming, we are waiting for the rule, reign, and reach of that kingdom to be fully realized. We *already* experience its effects in part, but have *not yet* tasted it in a complete form. Consider Heb 2:8-9, "at present we do not see everything subject to them [*not yet*]. But we do see Jesus, who was made lower than the angels for a little while, now crowned with glory and honor because he suffered death" [*already*]; I John 3:2, "Dear friends, now we are children of God, [*already*] and what we will be has not yet been made known. But we know that when Christ appears, we shall be like him, for we shall see him as he is." [*not yet*]; Rom 8:30 "those...he also glorified" [*already/not yet*]; and Eph 2:6 "God raised us up with Christ and seated us with him in the heavenly realms in Christ Jesus" [*already/not yet*].

[31] James M. Hamilton, *Work and Our Labor in the Lord: Short Studies in Biblical Theology* (Wheaton, IL: Crossway, 2017), 91.

[32] Amy Sherman offers preview passages that correlate with each one: Peace with God (*Intimacy with God*—Zeph 3:14-20, 1 Cor 13:12; *Beauty*—Is 35, Is 60); Peace with Self (*Health/Wholeness*—Is 32:3-4, Is 35:6, Is 65:19; *Hope*—Ps 68:6, Ps 113:9, Is 42:3-4; *Comfort*—Is 54); Peace with Others (*Unity*—Is 25:6-9, Rev 7:9-20; *Security/Lack of Violence*—Ps 46:9, Mic 4:3, Ezek 34:27-28); Peace with the Created Order (*Economic Flourishing*—Mic 4:4, Is 65:21-22, Joel 3:18, Is 49:10; *Sustainability*—Is 51:3, Is 35:1-2, 7). Amy Sherman, *Kingdom Calling: Vocational Stewardship for the Common Good* (Downers Grove, IL: InterVarsity, 2011), 34-43.

[33] Wolters, *Creation Regained*, 44-45.

[34] Comer, *Garden City*, 138.

[35] James K. A. Smith, *You Are What You Love: The Spiritual Power of Habit* (Grand Rapids: Brazos Press, 2016), 138.

[36] Os Guinness, *The Call: Finding and Fulfilling the Central Purpose of Your Life* (Nashville: W Publishing Group), 1998, 4.

[37] Ibid., 48-49.

[38] Gene C. Fant, Jr. *The Liberal Arts: A Student's Guide* (Wheaton, IL: Crossway, 2012), 25.

[39] Ibid., 40.

[40] Ibid., 41.

[41] Thomas Hine, *The Rise and Fall of the American Teenager* (New York: Perennial, 2000), 149.

[42] Fant Jr., *The Liberal Arts*, 19.

[43] Smith, *You Are What You Love*, 139.

[44] Ibid., 164.

[45] Charles Taylor, *The Ethics of Authenticity*, first ed. (Cambridge, MA: Harvard University Press, 1992), 40.

[46] Ibid., 29.

[47] Ibid.

[48] Taylor, *Ethics of Authenticity*, 40-41.

[49] Thomas À Kempis, "How Truth Instructs Us in Silence (III.2)," In *The Imitation of Christ*, translated by Leo Sherley-Price (London: Penguin Books, 1418/1952), 93.

[50] Robert Robinson, *Come Thou Fount of Every Blessing*, 1758.

[51] Jeffrey Jensen Arnett, *Emerging Adulthood: The Winding Road from the Late Teens through the Twenties*, second ed. (New York: Oxford University Press, 2014), 9.

[52] Jari-Erik Nurmi, "Socialization and Self-Development: Channeling, Selection, Adjustment, and Reflection." In *Handbook of Adolescent Psychology*, 2nd ed. (Hoboken: Wiley, 2004), 85.

[53] Arnett, *Emerging Adulthood*, 9.

[54] Irving B. Weiner, Richard M. Lerner, M. Ann Easterbrooks, Jayanthi Mistry, and Irving Weiner, eds. *Handbook of Psychology: Developmental Psychology* (Somerset: Wiley, 2012), 340.

[55] Not all teens may have this freedom to experiment. Some may feel shut out from exploring their identities because of their past experiences and life circumstances. They may struggle to see themselves as anything other than abused, unloved, forgotten, mentally ill, or marginalized. The good news

of the gospel speaks to these students as well. They are not their past. They are not their circumstances. They are beloved children of God, created on purpose and for a purpose.

56 Steven Garber, *Visions of Vocation: Common Grace for the Common Good* (Downers Grove, IL: IVP Books, 2014), 111.

57 Jeffrey Jensen Arnett, *Adolescence and Emerging Adulthood: A Cultural Approach*, second edition (Upper Saddle River, NJ: Prentice Hall, 2004).

58 Christian Smith, *Soul Searching: The Religious and Spiritual Lives of American Teenagers* (Oxford: Oxford University Press, 2005).

59 Chap Clark, *Hurt 2.0: Inside the World of Today's Teenagers* (Grand Rapids: Baker Academic, 2011). Patricia Hersch, *A Tribe Apart: A Journey Into the Heart of American Adolescents* (New York: Ballantine Books, 1998).

60 F. L. Cross, and E. A. Livingstone (Eds.) in *The Oxford dictionary of the Christian Church*, third ed. (New York: Oxford University Press, 2005), 994.

61 Richard J. Foster, *Celebration of Discipline*, Special Anniversary Edition (HarperOne: Kindle Edition), 105.

62 James K. A. Smith, *Desiring the Kingdom (Cultural Liturgies): Worship, Worldview, and Cultural Formation* (Grand Rapids: Baker Academic, 2009).

63 James K. A. Smith, *You Are What You Love: The Spiritual Power of Habit* (Baker Publishing Group. Kindle Edition), 37.

64 Kathryn Ecklund, Stephen Lambert, Cheryl Crawford, and Chris Neal (2018). Adolescent Depression, Anxiety, and Self Harm. *Youth Leadership Initiative*, 1(1). Azusa, CA: Azusa Pacific University Center for Vocational Ministry.

65 Smith, *You Are What You Love*, 7.

66 Ibid., 7.

67 Ibid., 1.

68 Ibid., 19.

69 Smith, *You Are What You Love*, 55-56.

70 Julie Singleton, "Head, Heart and Hands Model for Transformative Learning: Place as Context for Changing Sustainability Values," *Journal of Sustainability Education* 9 (March 2015). http://www.jsedimensions.org/wordpress/wp-content/uploads/2015/03/PDF-Singleton-JSE-March-2015-Love-Issue.pdf.

71 Bruce Lee was a Hong Kong-American actor, director, martial artist, martial

arts instructor, and philosopher.

[72] Kara Powell, Jake Mulder, and Brad. M. Griffin, *Growing Young: Six Essential Strategies to Help Young People Discover and Love Your Church* (Grand Rapids, MI: Baker Books, 2016).

[73] Ross A. Thompson, "Changing Societies, Changing Childhood: Studying the Impact of Globalization on Child Development," *Child Development Perspectives,* 187-192.

[74] Andy Crouch, *Culture Making: Recovering Our Creative Calling* (Downers Grove, IL: IVP Press, 2008).

[75] Jerusha O. Conner and Katherine Cosner, 2016. "Youth Change Agents: Comparing the Sociopolitical Identities of Youth Organizers and Youth Commissioners," *Democracy and Education.* 24, no. 2: 1-12.

[76] Cole and Durham (Eds.), *Figuring the Future: Children, Youth, and Globalization* (Santa Fe, NM: SAR Press, 2008) chapter 5.

[77] Forbes 2016 online article: https://www.forbes.com/sites/causeintegration/2016/11/28/get-ready-for-generation-z/#13173daa2204

[78] Brooke Lusk, "Digital Natives and Social Media Behaviors: An Overview," *The Prevention Researcher,* vol. 17, Supplement, 3-6.

[79] Crystal Kirgiss, *In Search of Adolescence: A New Look at an Old Idea,* (San Diego, CA: The Youth Cartel, 2015).

[80] Gabe Lyons, *The Next Christians: How A New Generation is Restoring the Faith,* (New York, NY: Doubleday, 2010).

[81] Barna Group, "How Teens Spend Their After School Hours," https://www.barna.com/research/teens-spend-school-hours/.

[82] Richard J. Foster, *Prayer* (San Francisco, CA: HarperCollins Publishers, 2002). And Gerald W. Peterman and Andrew J. Schmutzer, *Between Pain and Grace: A Biblical Theology of Suffering* (Chicago, IL: Moody Publishers, 2016).

[83] Foster, *Prayer,* 208.

[84] Michalinos Zembylas, "The 'Crisis of Pity' and the Radicalization of Solidarity: Toward Critical Pedagogies of Compassion," *Educational Studies,* issue 49, 504-521.

[85] Gustavo Gutierrez, *A Theology of Liberation: History, Politics, and Salvation* (Maryknoll, NY: Orbis Books, 1973).

[86] "A Christian Vision for Flourishing Communities," A Resource
from the Oikonomia Network.

[87] William Isaacs, *Dialogue: The Art of Thinking Together* (New York: DoubleDay,
1999), 19.

[88] To cultivate love for neighbor as ourselves we must understand our neighbor.

[89] Listening: Genuinely trying to understand another person without resistance
or imposition; no interrupting. Respecting: Validating the integrity of another
person's position or opinion. Suspending Judgment: Separating the person
from his/her opinions; no judgment of person. Voicing: Speaking the truth
of one's own authority, who one really is and thinks. (These definitions were
adapted from William Isaac's book, *Dialogue: The Art of Thinking Together,*
New York: DoubleDay, 1999).

[90] Thomas Hine, *The Rise and Fall of the American Teenager*
(New York: Perennial, 2000), 154.